MACBETH

WITH READER'S GUIDE

AMSCO LITERATURE PROGRAM

WILBERT J. LEVY, *Program Editor*

William Shakespeare

MACBETH

Amsco Literature Program

When ordering this book, you may specify:
R 132 ALP (Paperback)
R 132 H (Hardbound)

WITH READER'S GUIDE

Solomon Schlakman

Amsco School Publications, Inc.
315 HUDSON STREET NEW YORK, N.Y. 10013

ISBN 0-87720-803-4 (Paperback)
ISBN 0-87720-835-2 (Hardbound)

Macbeth with Reader's Guide

Printed in the United States of America

CONTENTS

Characters in the Play

Duncan, king of Scotland

Malcolm
Donalbain } his sons

Macbeth
Banquo } generals of the King's army

Macduff
Lennox
Ross
Menteith } noblemen of Scotland
Angus
Caithness

Fleance, son to Banquo
Siward, earl of Northumberland, general of the English forces
Young Siward, his son
Seyton, an officer attending on Macbeth
Boy, son to Macduff
An English Doctor
A Scotch Doctor
A Sergeant
A Porter
An Old Man

Lady Macbeth
Lady Macduff
Gentlewoman attending on Lady Macbeth

Hecate
Three Witches
Apparitions

Lords, Gentlemen, Officers, Soldiers, Murderers, Attendants, and
Messengers

The Tragedy of Macbeth

9, 10 Graymalkin, Paddock names given to the "familiars" of the witches. Familiars were evil spirits who took possession of old women and made witches of them. Graymalkin was a name for a cat; Paddock, for a toad. Witches had limited powers of their own, but had to obey their familiars.

ACT I

Scene 1. A desert place

Thunder and Lightning. Enter three Witches.

First Witch
  When shall we three meet again
  In thunder, lightning, or in rain?
Second Witch
  When the hurlyburly's done,
  When the battle's lost and won.
Third Witch
  That will be ere the set of sun.
First Witch
  Where the place?
Second Witch
                  Upon the heath.
Third Witch
  There to meet with Macbeth.
First Witch
  I come, Graymalkin.
All
  Paddock calls—anon!
  Fair is foul, and foul is fair.
  Hover through the fog and filthy air.
                              [*Exeunt.*

3

4 sergeant the equivalent of a modern captain.

15 kerns lightly armed foot soldiers.
gallowglasses specially picked and expert soldiers.

21 minion a favorite or darling.

24 unseam'd ripped open.
nave navel.
chaps jaws.

Scene 2. A camp near Forres

Alarum within. Enter Duncan, Malcolm, Donal-bain, Lennox, with Attendants, meeting a bleeding Sergeant.

Duncan
  What bloody man is that? He can report,
  As seemeth by his plight, of the revolt
  The newest state.

Malcolm
                    This is the sergeant
  Who like a good and hardy soldier fought   5
  'Gainst my captivity. Hail, brave friend!
  Say to the king the knowledge of the broil
  As thou didst leave it.

Sergeant
                    Doubtful it stood;
  As two spent swimmers, that do cling together   10
  And choke their art. The merciless Macdonwald—
  Worthy to be a rebel, for to that
  The multiplying villainies of nature
  Do swarm upon him—from the western isles
  Of kerns and gallowglasses is supplied;   15
  And fortune, on his damned quarrel smiling,
  Show'd like a rebel's whore: but all's too weak:
  For brave Macbeth—well he deserves that name—
  Disdaining fortune, with his brandish'd steel
  Which smok'd with bloody execution,   20
  Like valor's minion carv'd out his passage
  Till he fac'd the slave;
  Which ne'er shook hands, nor bade farewell to him,
  Till he unseam'd him from the nave to the chaps,
  And fix'd his head upon our battlements.   25

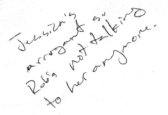

33 surveying vantage seeing an opportunity to attack.

44 memorize another Golgotha make the place as horribly memorable as Golgotha. The biblical Golgotha was the scene of Christ's crucifixion, a site marked with the skulls and bones of those crucified there.

50 thane a title of nobility in Scotland.

Duncan

O valiant cousin! worthy gentleman!

Sergeant

As whence the sun 'gins his reflection
Shipwrecking storms and direful thunders break,
So from that spring whence comfort seem'd to come
Discomfort swells. Mark, king of Scotland, mark: 30
No sooner justice had, with valor arm'd,
Compell'd these skipping kerns to trust their heels,
But the Norweyan lord, surveying vantage,
With furbish'd arms and new supplies of men,
Began a fresh assault.   35

Duncan

                Dismay'd not this
Our captains, Macbeth and Banquo?

Sergeant

                        Yes;
As sparrows eagles, or the hare the lion.
If I say sooth, I must report they were   40
As cannons overcharg'd with double cracks; so they
Doubly redoubled strokes upon the foe:
Except they meant to bathe in reeking wounds,
Or memorize another Golgotha,
I cannot tell—   45
But I am faint; my gashes cry for help.

Duncan

So well thy words become thee as thy wounds;
They smack of honor both. Go get him surgeons.
                [*Exit Sergeant, attended.*
Who comes here?

    Enter Ross.

Malcolm

                The worthy thane of Ross.   50

Lennox

What a haste looks through his eyes! So should he look
That seems to speak things strange.

61 **Bellona's bridegroom** a reference to Macbeth as, metaphor-
ically, the husband of the Roman goddess of war, Bellona.
In many myths Bellona's husband was Mars.
lapp'd in proof clothed in strong armor.

68 **composition** terms of peace.

Ross

                              God save the king!

Duncan
  Whence cam'st thou, worthy thane?

Ross

                              From Fife, great king;   55
  Where the Norweyan banners flout the sky
  And fan our people cold. Norway himself
  With terrible numbers,
  Assisted by that most disloyal traitor
  The thane of Cawdor, began a dismal conflict;   60
  Till that Bellona's bridegroom, lapp'd in proof,
  Confronted him with self-comparisons,
  Point against point rebellious, arm 'gainst arm,
  Curbing his lavish spirit: and, to conclude,
  The victory fell on us.   65

Duncan
                              Great happiness!

Ross
  That now
  Sweno, the Norway's king, craves composition;
  Nor would we deign him burial of his men
  Till he disbursed, at Saint Colme's inch,   70
  Ten thousand dollars to our general use.

Duncan
  No more that thane of Cawdor shall deceive
  Our bosom interest: go pronounce his present death,
  And with his former title greet Macbeth.

Ross
  I'll see it done.   75

Duncan
  What he hath lost, noble Macbeth hath won.
                                        [*Exeunt.*

6 Aroint thee Off with you!
  ronyon good-for-nothing – a term of contempt.

16 quarters points.
17 shipman's card navigator's compass.

Scene 3. A heath

Thunder. Enter the three Witches.

First Witch
  Where hast thou been, sister?
Second Witch
  Killing swine.
Third Witch
  Sister, where thou?
First Witch
  A sailor's wife had chestnuts in her lap,
  And mounch'd, and mounch'd, and mounch'd. "Give   5
      me," quoth I:
  "Aroint thee, witch!" the rump-fed ronyon cries.
  Her husband's to Aleppo gone, master o' the Tiger;
  But in a sieve I'll thither sail,
  And, like a rat without a tail,
  I'll do, I'll do, and I'll do.   10
Second Witch
  I'll give thee a wind.
First Witch
  Thou 'rt kind.
Third Witch
  And I another.
First Witch
  I myself have all the other;
  And the very ports they blow,   15
  All the quarters that they know
  I' the shipman's card.
  I will drain him dry as hay:
  Sleep shall neither night nor day
  Hang upon his pent-house lid;   20
  He shall live a man forbid:
  Weary sev'nights nine times nine

44 **choppy** chapped or cracked.

Shall he dwindle, peak, and pine:
Though his bark cannot be lost,
Yet it shall be tempest-tost.   25
Look what I have.

Second Witch
Show me, show me.

First Witch
Here I have a pilot's thumb,
Wreck'd as homeward he did come.

[*Drum within.*

Third Witch
A drum, a drum!   30
Macbeth doth come.

All
The weird sisters, hand in hand,
Posters of the sea and land,
Thus do go about, about:
Thrice to thine, and thrice to mine,   35
And thrice again, to make up nine.
Peace! the charm's wound up.

Enter Macbeth and Banquo.

Macbeth
So foul and fair a day I have not seen.

Banquo
How far is't call'd to Forres? What are these
So wither'd, and so wild in their attire,   40
That look not like th' inhabitants o' the earth,
And yet are on 't? Live you? or are you aught
That man may question? You seem to understand me,
By each at once her choppy finger laying
Upon her skinny lips: you should be women,   45
And yet your beards forbid me to interpret
That you are so.

Macbeth
                Speak, if you can: what are you?

49   **thane of Glamis** the title Macbeth had recently inherited on the death of his father.

52   **why do you start** why are you startled?

First Witch
    All hail, Macbeth! hail to thee, thane of Glamis!

Second Witch
    All hail, Macbeth! hail to thee, thane of Cawdor!   50

Third Witch
    All hail, Macbeth, thou shalt be king hereafter!

Banquo
    Good sir, why do you start, and seem to fear
    Things that do sound so fair? I' the name of truth,
    Are ye fantastical, or that indeed
    Which outwardly ye show? My noble partner   55
    You greet with present grace and great prediction
    Of noble having and of royal hope,
    That he seems rapt withal: to me you speak not:
    If you can look into the seeds of time,
    And say which grain will grow and which will not,   60
    Speak then to me, who neither beg nor fear
    Your favors nor your hate.

First Witch
    Hail!

Second Witch
    Hail!

Third Witch
    Hail!   65

First Witch
    Lesser than Macbeth, and greater.

Second Witch
    Not so happy, yet much happier.

Third Witch
    Thou shalt get kings, though thou be none:
    So all hail, Macbeth and Banquo!

First Witch
    Banquo and Macbeth, all hail!   70

Macbeth
    Stay, you imperfect speakers, tell me more:

82   **corporal**   possessing a body; substantial.

85   **insane root**   some plant that causes insanity.

By Sinel's death I know I am thane of Glamis;
But how of Cawdor? the thane of Cawdor lives,
A prosperous gentleman; and to be king
Stands not within the prospect of belief,   75
No more than to be Cawdor. Say from whence
You owe this strange intelligence? or why
Upon this blasted heath you stop our way
With such prophetic greeting? Speak, I charge you.
                              [*Witches vanish.*

Banquo
The earth hath bubbles as the water has,   80
And these are of them: whither are they vanish'd?

Macbeth
Into the air, and what seem'd corporal melted
As breath into the wind. Would they had stay'd!

Banquo
Were such things here as we do speak about?
Or have we eaten on the insane root   85
That takes the reason prisoner?

Macbeth
Your children shall be kings.

Banquo
                              You shall be king.

Macbeth
And thane of Cawdor too: went it not so?

Banquo
To the selfsame tune and words. Who's here?   90

        Enter Ross and Angus.

Ross
The king hath happily receiv'd, Macbeth,
The news of thy success: and when he reads
Thy personal venture in the rebels' fight,
His wonders and his praises do contend
Which should be thine or his: silenc'd with that,   95
In viewing o'er the rest o' the selfsame day,

100   **post with post**   messenger after messenger.

123   **behind**   yet to come.

He finds thee in the stout Norweyan ranks,
Nothing afeard of what thyself didst make,
Strange images of death. As thick as hail
Came post with post, and every one did bear   100
Thy praises in his kingdom's great defense,
And pour'd them down before him.

Angus

                                        We are sent
To give thee, from our royal master, thanks;
Only to herald thee into his sight,   105
Not pay thee.

Ross

And for an earnest of a greater honor,
He bade me, from him, call thee thane of Cawdor:
In which addition, hail, most worthy thane!
For it is thine.   110

Banquo

                    What, can the devil speak true?

Macbeth

The thane of Cawdor lives: why do you dress me
In borrow'd robes?

Angus

                    Who was the thane lives yet,
But under heavy judgment bears that life   115
Which he deserves to lose. Whether he was combin'd
With those of Norway, or did line the rebel
With hidden help and vantage, or that with both
He labor'd in his country's wreck, I know not;
But treasons capital, confess'd and prov'd,   120
Have overthrown him.

Macbeth

          [*Aside*]   Glamis, and thane of Cawdor:
The greatest is behind.—Thanks for your pains.—
Do you not hope your children shall be kings,
When those that gave the thane of Cawdor to me   125
Promis'd no less to them?

138 **soliciting** tempting.

140 **earnest** promise, evidence

143 **unfix my hair** make my hair stand on end.

147 **fantastical** imaginary.

148—149 **function / Is smother'd in surmise** Powers of thought and action are incapable of functioning because of imagination.

152 **chance may crown me** The crown in Scotland was elective. On the death of the king, the nobles elected someone of royal blood to succeed, unless the king had specifically indicated his successor, in which case the nobles were likely to carry out the king's wish. Macbeth feels here he would be elected to succeed Duncan, since he is of royal blood and has distinguished himself.

Banquo

That, trusted home,
Might yet enkindle you unto the crown,
Besides the thane of Cawdor. But 'tis strange;
And oftentimes, to win us to our harm,   130
The instruments of darkness tell us truths,
Win us with honest trifles, to betray 's
In deepest consequence.
Cousins, a word, I pray you.

Macbeth

[*Aside*]   Two truths are told,   135
As happy prologues to the swelling act
Of the imperial theme.—I thank you, gentlemen.—
[*Aside*]   This supernatural soliciting
Cannot be ill; cannot be good: if ill,
Why hath it given me earnest of success,   140
Commencing in a truth? I am thane of Cawdor:
If good, why do I yield to that suggestion
Whose horrid image doth unfix my hair
And make my seated heart knock at my ribs,
Against the use of nature? Present fears   145
Are less than horrible imaginings:
My thought, whose murder yet is but fantastical,
Shakes so my single state of man that function
Is smother'd in surmise, and nothing is
But what is not.   150

Banquo

Look, how our partner's rapt.

Macbeth

[*Aside*]   If chance will have me king, why, chance may
crown me,
Without my stir.

Banquo

New honors come upon him,
Like our strange garments, cleave not to their mold   155
But with the aid of use.

157 Come what come may another expression of Macbeth's decision to leave his future to chance.

Macbeth
            [*Aside*]   Come what come may,
    Time and the hour runs through the roughest day.

Banquo
    Worthy Macbeth, we stay upon your leisure.

Macbeth
    Give me your favor: my dull brain was wrought   160
    With things forgotten. Kind gentlemen, your pains
    Are register'd where every day I turn
    The leaf to read them. Let us toward the king.
    Think upon what hath chanc'd, and at more time,
    The interim having weigh'd it, let us speak   165
    Our free hearts each to other.

Banquo
                            Very gladly.

Macbeth
    Till then, enough. Come, friends.
                                    [*Exeunt.*

Scene 4. Forres. The palace
~~~~~~~~~~~~~~~~~~~~~~~~

Flourish. Enter Duncan, Malcolm, Donalbain,
Lennox, and Attendants.

Duncan
    Is execution done on Cawdor? Are not
    Those in commission yet return'd?

Malcolm
                            My liege,
    They are not yet come back. But I have spoke
    With one that saw him die, who did report   5
    That very frankly he confess'd his treasons,

10 **studied** prepared carefully.

32–33 The reward Duncan has given Macbeth is only the first in
a number of others to come.

Implor'd your highness' pardon and set forth
A deep repentance: nothing in his life
Became him like the leaving it; he died
As one that had been studied in his death,   10
To throw away the dearest thing he ow'd
As 'twere a careless trifle.

Duncan
                              There's no art
To find the mind's construction in the face:
He was a gentleman on whom I built   15
An absolute trust.

Enter Macbeth, Banquo, Ross, and Angus.

                    O worthiest cousin!
The sin of my ingratitude even now
Was heavy on me: thou art so far before,
That swiftest wing of recompense is slow   20
To overtake thee. Would thou hadst less deserv'd,
That the proportion both of thanks and payment
Might have been mine! only I have left to say,
More is thy due than more than all can pay.

Macbeth
The service and the loyalty I owe,   25
In doing it, pays itself. Your highness' part
Is to receive our duties: and our duties
Are to your throne and state children and servants;
Which do but what they should, by doing every thing
Safe toward your love and honor.   30

Duncan
                         Welcome hither:
I have begun to plant thee, and will labor
To make thee full of growing. Noble Banquo,
That hast no less deserv'd, nor must be known
No less to have done so: let me infold thee   35
And hold thee to my heart.

43–45   Duncan designates Malcolm to be his choice to succeed to the throne — a blow to Macbeth's expectations.

48   **Inverness**   Macbeth's castle.

51   **harbinger**   an officer who goes ahead to arrange lodgings for the king.

Banquo
                           There if I grow
  The harvest is your own.
Duncan
                           My plenteous joys,
    Wanton in fullness, seek to hide themselves   40
    In drops of sorrow. Sons, kinsmen, thanes,
    And you whose places are the nearest, know,
    We will establish our estate upon
    Our eldest, Malcolm, whom we name hereafter
    The Prince of Cumberland: which honor must   45
    Not unaccompanied invest him only,
    But signs of nobleness, like stars, shall shine
    On all deservers. From hence to Inverness,
    And bind us further to you.
Macbeth
    The rest is labor, which is not us'd for you: 50
    I'll be myself the harbinger, and make joyful
    The hearing of my wife with your approach;
    So humbly take my leave.
Duncan
                           My worthy Cawdor!
Macbeth
    [Aside]   The Prince of Cumberland! that is a step   55
    On which I must fall down, or else o'erleap,
    For in my way it lies. Stars, hide your fires;
    Let not light see my black and deep desires:
    The eye wink at the hand; yet let that be
    Which the eye fears, when it is done, to see.   60
                                   [Exit.

Duncan
    True, worthy Banquo; he is full so valiant,
    And in his commendations I am fed;
    It is a banquet to me. Let's after him,
    Whose care is gone before to bid us welcome:
    It is a peerless kinsman.   65
                           [Flourish. Exeunt.

27 chastise suppress.
28 golden round the crown.
29 metaphysical supernatural.

Scene 5. *Inverness. Macbeth's castle*

Enter Lady Macbeth, reading a letter.

Lady Macbeth
    "They met me in the day of success; and I have
    learned by the perfectest report, they have more in
    them than mortal knowledge. When I burned in de-
    sire to question them further, they made themselves
    air, into which they vanished. Whiles I stood rapt   5
    in the wonder of it, came missives from the king, who
    all-hailed me 'Thane of Cawdor'; by which title, be-
    fore, these weird sisters saluted me, and referred me
    to the coming on of time, with 'Hail, king that
    shalt be!' This have I thought good to deliver thee,   10
    my dearest partner of greatness, that thou mightst
    not lose the dues of rejoicing, by being ignorant of
    what greatness is promised thee. Lay it to thy heart,
    and farewell."

    Glamis thou art, and Cawdor, and shalt be   15
    What thou art promis'd: yet do I fear thy nature;
    It is too full o' the milk of human kindness
    To catch the nearest way: thou wouldst be great;
    Are not without ambition, but without
    The illness should attend it: what thou wouldst highly,   20
    That wouldst thou holily; wouldst not play false,
    And yet wouldst wrongly win; thou'dst have, great
          Glamis,
    That which cries "Thus thou must do, if thou have it;
    And that which rather thou dost fear to do
    Than wishest should be undone." Hie thee hither,   25
    That I may pour my spirits in thine ear,
    And chastise with the valor of my tongue
    All that impedes thee from the golden round,
    Which fate and metaphysical aid doth seem

49   **compunctious visitings of nature** natural promptings or qualms of conscience.
50   **fell** evil, cruel.

50–51   **keep peace between / Th' effect and it** come between my purpose and its fulfilment.
52   **gall** the bitter secretion of the liver.
55   **pall** cover up, enshroud.
      dunnest darkest.

To have thee crown'd withal.

    Enter a Messenger.

                           What is your tidings?

Messenger
The king comes here tonight.

Lady Macbeth
                     Thou 'rt mad to say it:
Is not thy master with him? who, were 't so,
Would have inform'd for preparation.   35

Messenger
So please you, it is true: our thane is coming:
One of my fellows had the speed of him,
Who, almost dead for breath, had scarcely more
Than would make up his message.

Lady Macbeth   — *speech goes with*
        Macbeth's on p. 39 Give him tending;   40
He brings great news.
                          [*Exit Messenger.*
             The raven himself is hoarse
That croaks the fatal entrance of Duncan
Under my battlements. Come, you spirits
That tend on mortal thoughts, unsex me here,   45
And fill me, from the crown to the toe, top-full
Of direst cruelty! make thick my blood,
Stop up th' access and passage to remorse,
That no compunctious visitings of nature
Shake my fell purpose, nor keep peace between   50
Th' effect and it! Come to my woman's breasts,
And take my milk for gall, you murd'ring ministers,
Wherever in your sightless substances
You wait on nature's mischief! Come, thick night,
And pall thee in the dunnest smoke of hell,   55
That my keen knife see not the wound it makes,
Nor heaven peep through the blanket of the dark,
To cry "Hold, hold!"

71 **beguile** deceive.

76 **dispatch** management.

81 **To alter favor is to fear** When one displays an unaccus-
tomed countenance, he appears to be fearful of something.

Enter Macbeth.

                    Great Glamis! worthy Cawdor!
Greater than both, by the all-hail hereafter!   60
Thy letters have transported me beyond
This ignorant present, and I feel now
The future in the instant.

Macbeth
                    My dearest love,
Duncan comes here tonight.   65

Lady Macbeth
                      And when goes hence?

Macbeth
Tomorrow, as he purposes.

Lady Macbeth
                    O, never
Shall sun that morrow see!
Your face, my thane, is as a book where men   70
May read strange matters. To beguile the time,
Look like the time; bear welcome in your eye,
Your hand, your tongue: look like the innocent flower,
But be the serpent under 't. He that's coming
Must be provided for: and you shall put   75
This night's great business into my dispatch;
Which shall to all our nights and days to come
Give solely sovereign sway and masterdom.

Macbeth
We will speak further.

Lady Macbeth
                Only look up clear;   80
To alter favor ever is to fear:
Leave all the rest to me.
                            [*Exeunt.*

5 **temple-haunting martlet** The martlet was a bird that generally built its nest around churches; it was considered a bird of good omen.

6 **mansionry** abode, referring to the nests of the birds.

9 **procreant** breeding.

23 **hermits** dependents.

Scene 6. Before Macbeth's castle

Hautboys and torches. Enter Duncan, Malcolm, Donalbain, Banquo, Lennox, Macduff, Ross, Angus, and Attendants.

Duncan

    This castle hath a pleasant seat; the air
    Nimbly and sweetly recommends itself
    Unto our gentle senses.

Banquo

                This guest of summer,
    The temple-haunting martlet, does approve   5
    By his lov'd mansionry that the heaven's breath
    Smells wooingly here: no jutty, frieze,
    Buttress, nor coign of vantage, but this bird
    Hath made his pendant bed and procreant cradle:
    Where they most breed and haunt, I have observ'd   10
    The air is delicate.

    Enter Lady Macbeth.

Duncan

              See, see, our honor'd hostess!
    The love that follows us sometime is our trouble,
    Which still we thank as love. Herein I teach you
    How you shall bid God 'ild us for your pains,   15
    And thank us for your trouble.

Lady Macbeth

              All our service
    In every point twice done, and then done double.
    Were poor and single business to contend
    Against those honors deep and broad wherewith   20
    Your majesty loads our house: for those of old,
    And the late dignities heap'd up to them,
    We rest your hermits.

26 **purveyor** the officer who makes advance arrangements for an army. Duncan indicates the esteem he has for Macbeth; he would himself be the purveyor for his general.

31 **in compt** in trust for the king.

3 **trammel up** catch, as in a net.
4 **his surcease** Duncan's end or death.

6 **this bank and shoal of time** this world.

Duncan

                   Where's the thane of Cawdor?
We cours'd him at the heels, and had a purpose   25
To be his purveyor: but he rides well,
And his great love, sharp as his spur, hath holp him
To his home before us. Fair and noble hostess,
We are your guest tonight.

Lady Macbeth

                       Your servants ever   30
Have theirs, themselves, and what is theirs, in compt,
To make their audit at your highness' pleasure,
Still to return your own.

Duncan

                  Give me your hand;
Conduct me to mine host: we love him highly,   35
And shall continue our graces towards him.
By your leave, hostess.

                          [*Exeunt.*

Scene 7. *Macbeth's castle*

*Hautboys and torches. Enter a Sewer, and divers
Servants with dishes and service, and pass over the
stage. Then enter Macbeth.*

Macbeth

If it were done when 'tis done, then 'twere well
It were done quickly: if th' assassination
Could trammel up the consequence, and catch,
With his surcease, success; that but this blow
Might be the be-all and the end-all here,   5
But here, upon this bank and shoal of time,
We'd jump the life to come. But in these cases

11 chalice   cup.

22 cherubin   angels.
23 sightless   invisible.

We still have judgment here; that we but teach
Bloody instructions, which being taught return
To plague th' inventor: this even-handed justice   10
Commends the ingredients of our poison'd chalice
To our own lips. He's here in double trust:
First, as I am his kinsman and his subject,
Strong both against the deed; then, as his host,
Who should against his murderer shut the door,   15
Not bear the knife myself. Besides, this Duncan
Hath borne his faculties so meek, hath been
So clear in his great office, that his virtues
Will plead like angels trumpet-tongued against
The deep damnation of his taking-off;   20
And pity, like a naked new-born babe,
Striding the blast, or heaven's cherubin hors'd
Upon the sightless couriers of the air,
Shall blow the horrid deed in every eye,
That tears shall drown the wind. I have no spur   25
To prick the sides of my intent, but only
Vaulting ambition, which o'erleaps itself
And falls on the other.

    Enter Lady Macbeth.

                   How now! what news?

Lady Macbeth
He has almost supp'd: why have you left the chamber?   30

Macbeth
Hath he ask'd for me?

Lady Macbeth
              Know you not he has?

Macbeth
We will proceed no further in this business:
He hath honor'd me of late; and I have bought
Golden opinions from all sorts of people,   35
Which would be worn now in their newest gloss,
Not cast aside so soon.

48 poor cat a reference to a cat in a popular proverb who would hold back from eating fish for fear of wetting its feet.

53 break this enterprise   propose this idea.

57 Did then adhere   was then suitable.

Lady Macbeth
              Was the hope drunk
Wherein you dress'd yourself? hath it slept since?
And wakes it now, to look so green and pale   40
At what it did so freely? From this time
Such I account thy love. Art thou afeard
To be the same in thine own act and valor
As thou art in desire? Wouldst thou have that
Which thou esteem'st the ornament of life, *crown,* 45
                                  kingship
And live a coward in thine own esteem,
Letting "I dare not" wait upon "I would,"
Like the poor cat i' th' adage?

Macbeth
                   Prithee, peace:
I dare do all that may become a man;   50
Who dares do more is none.

Lady Macbeth
                 What beast was 't then
That made you break this enterprise to me?
When you durst do it, then you were a man;
And, to be more than what you were, you would   55
Be so much more the man. Nor time nor place
Did then adhere, and yet you would make both:
They have made themselves, and that their fitness now
Does unmake you. I have given suck, and know
How tender 'tis to love the babe that milks me: *milk of* 60 *human*
I would, while it was smiling in my face,   *kindness.*
Have pluck'd my nipple from his boneless gums,
And dash'd the brains out, had I so sworn as you
Have done to this.

Macbeth
            If we should fail?   65

Lady Macbeth
                     We fail!
But screw your courage to the sticking-place.
And we'll not fail. When Duncan is asleep—

mean

71   **wassail** drinking.
      convince overpower.

74   **limbec** alembic, top part of apparatus for distilling alcohol.

79   **quell** killing.

81   **mettle** spirit, quality.

Whereto the rather shall his day's hard journey
Soundly invite him—his two chamberlains   70
Will I with wine and wassail so convince,
That memory, the warder of the brain,
Shall be a fume, and the receipt of reason
A limbec only: when in swinish sleep
Their drenched natures lie as in a death,   75
What cannot you and I perform upon
Th' unguarded Duncan? what not put upon
His spongy officers, who shall bear the guilt
Of our great quell?

Macbeth
              Bring forth men-children only;   80
For thy undaunted mettle should compose
Nothing but males. Will it not be receiv'd,
When we have mark'd with blood those sleepy two
Of his own chamber, and us'd their very daggers,
That they have done 't?   85

Lady Macbeth
          Who dares receive it other,
As we shall make our griefs and clamor roar
Upon his death?

Macbeth
        I am settled, and bend up
Each corporal agent to this terrible feat.   90
Away, and mock the time with fairest show:
False face must hide what the false heart doth know.
                        [*Exeunt.*

p.33
Lady Macbeth — some thro

5 husbandry thrift.

ACT II

Scene 1. Inverness. Court of Macbeth's castle

*Enter Banquo, and Fleance bearing a torch before
him.*

Banquo
How goes the night, boy?
Fleance
The moon is down; I have not heard the clock.
Banquo
And she goes down at twelve.
Fleance
                  I take 't, 'tis later, sir.
Banquo
Hold, take my sword. There's husbandry in heaven,   5
Their candles are all out. Take thee that too.
A heavy summons lies like lead upon me,
And yet I would not sleep. Merciful powers,
Restrain in me the cursed thoughts that nature
Gives way to in repose!   10

  Enter Macbeth, and a Servant with a torch.

                  Give me my sword.
Who's there?
Macbeth
A friend.
Banquo
What, sir, not yet at rest? The king's a-bed:
He hath been in unusual pleasure, and   15

16 **great largess to your offices** gifts sent to the quarters of Macbeth's servants.

18–19 **shut up / In measureless content** Duncan concluded with expressions of great contentment.

31 **cleave to my consent** join with me.
when 'tis when the right time comes.

35 **bosom franchis'd** my heart free of sin or guilt.

Sent forth great largess to your offices:
This diamond he greets your wife withal,
By the name of most kind hostess; and shut up
In measureless content.

Macbeth

                        Being unprepar'd,   20
Our will became the servant to defect,
Which else should free have wrought.

Banquo

                                All's well.
I dreamt last night of the three weird sisters:
To you they have show'd some truth.   25

Macbeth

                            I think not of them:
Yet, when we can entreat an hour to serve,
We would spend it in some words upon that business,
If you would grant the time.

Banquo

                            At your kind'st leisure.   30

Macbeth

If you shall cleave to my consent, when 'tis,
It shall make honor for you.

Banquo

                               So I lose none
In seeking to augment it, but still keep
My bosom franchis'd and allegiance clear,   35
I shall be counsel'd.

Macbeth

                        Good repose the while!

Banquo

Thanks, sir: the like to you!
                    [Exeunt Banquo and Fleance.

Macbeth

Go bid thy mistress, when my drink is ready,
She strike upon the bell. Get thee to bed.   40

48 **palpable** tangible.

50 **marshal'st** leads.

54 **dudgeon** handle.

60 **Hecate** goddess of witchcraft.
61 **Alarum'd** called to action.

63 **Tarquin** Roman tyrant who raped Lucrece as she slept.

[*Exit Servant.*

Is this a dagger which I see before me,
The handle toward my hand? Come, let me clutch
     thee.
I have thee not, and yet I see thee still.
Art thou not, fatal vision, sensible
To feeling as to sight? or art thou but   45
A dagger of the mind, a false creation,
Proceeding from the heat-oppressed brain?
I see thee yet, in form as palpable
As this which now I draw.
Thou marshal'st me the way that I was going;   50
And such an instrument I was to use.
Mine eyes are made the fools o' the other senses,
Or else worth all the rest: I see thee still;
And on thy blade and dudgeon gouts of blood,
Which was not so before. There's no such thing: 55
It is the bloody business which informs
Thus to mine eyes. Now o'er the one half-world
Nature seems dead, and wicked dreams abuse
The curtain'd sleep; witchcraft celebrates
Pale Hecate's offerings; and wither'd murder,   60
Alarum'd by his sentinel, the wolf,
Whose howl's his watch, thus with his stealthy pace,
With Tarquin's ravishing strides, towards his design
Moves like a ghost. Thou sure and firm-set earth,
Hear not my steps, which way they walk, for fear   65
Thy very stones prate of my whereabout,
And take the present horror from the time,
Which now suits with it. Whiles I threat, he lives:
Words to the heat of deeds too cold breath gives.

[A *bell rings.*

I go, and it is done: the bell invites me.   70
Hear it not, Duncan, for it is a knell
That summons thee to heaven, or to hell.

[*Exit.*

3 **fatal bellman** the town crier who tolled the bell on the night before an execution.

6 **possets** hot drinks.

Scene 2. The same

Enter Lady Macbeth.

Lady Macbeth.
    That which hath made them drunk hath made me
        bold;
    What hath quench'd them hath given me fire. Hark!
        Peace!
    It was the owl that shriek'd, the fatal bellman,
    Which gives the stern'st good-night. He is about it:
    The doors are open, and the surfeited grooms   5
    Do mock their charge with snores. I have drugg'd
        their possets,
    That death and nature do contend about them,
    Whether they live or die.
Macbeth.
                [*Within*]   Who's there? what, ho?
Lady Macbeth
    Alack, I am afraid they have awak'd   10
    And 'tis not done: th' attempt and not the deed
    Confounds us. Hark! I laid their daggers ready;
    He could not miss 'em. Had he not resembled
    My father as he slept, I had done 't.

    Enter Macbeth.

                                    My husband!   15
Macbeth
    I have done the deed. Didst thou not hear a noise?
Lady Macbeth
    I heard the owl scream and the crickets cry.
    Did not you speak?
Macbeth
                When?

26 **sorry** miserable, horrible.

34 **hangman's hands** the hangman was often required to cut up the body of an executed prisoner.

Lady Macbeth

　　　　　　　　　　Now.　　　　　　　　20

Macbeth

　　　　　　　　　　　As I descended?

Lady Macbeth
　Aye.

Macbeth
　Hark!
　Who lies i' the second chamber?

Lady Macbeth

　　　　　　　　　　　　Donalbain.　　　　　25

Macbeth
　This is a sorry sight.

　　　　　　　　　[Looking on his hands.

Lady Macbeth
　A foolish thought, to say a sorry sight.

Macbeth
　There's one did laugh in 's sleep, and one cried
　　　"Murder!"
　That they did wake each other: I stood and heard
　　　them:
　But they did say their prayers, and address'd them　　30
　Again to sleep.

Lady Macbeth
　　　　　　　　There are two lodged together.

Macbeth
　One cried "God bless us!" and "Amen" the other,
　As they had seen me with these hangman's hands:
　List'ning their fear, I could not say "Amen,"　　　35
　When they did say "God bless us!"

Lady Macbeth
　Consider it not so deeply.

Macbeth
　But wherefore could not I pronounce "Amen"?

45   **ravel'd sleave**   tangled skein (of thread).

I had most need of blessing, and "Amen"
Stuck in my throat.   40

Lady Macbeth

                These deeds must not be thought
After these ways; so, it will make us mad.

Macbeth

Methought I heard a voice cry "Sleep no more!
Macbeth does murder sleep"—the innocent sleep,
Sleep that knits up the ravel'd sleave of care,   45
The death of each day's life, sore labor's bath,
Balm of hurt minds, great nature's second course,
Chief nourisher in life's feast—

Lady Macbeth

                    What do you mean?

Macbeth

Still it cried "Sleep no more!" to all the house: 50
"Glamis hath murder'd sleep, and therefore Cawdor
Shall sleep no more: Macbeth shall sleep no more."

Lady Macbeth

Who was it that thus cried? Why, worthy thane,
You do unbend your noble strength, to think
So brainsickly of things. Go get some water,   55
And wash this filthy witness from your hand.
Why did you bring these daggers from the place?
They must lie there: go carry them, and smear
The sleepy grooms with blood.

Macbeth

                  I'll go no more: 60
I am afraid to think what I have done;
Look on 't again I dare not.

Lady Macbeth

                Infirm of purpose!
Give me the daggers: the sleeping and the dead
Are but as pictures: 'tis the eye of childhood   65
That fears a painted devil. If he do bleed,

67 **gild** smear.

74 **incarnadine** change to a deep-red color.

81 **constancy** composure.
82 **left you unattended** abandoned you.

85 **to be watchers** to have been awake.

I'll gild the faces of the grooms withal,
For it must seem their guilt.

                        [*Exit. Knocking within.*

Macbeth

                        Whence is that knocking?
How is 't with me, when every noise appals me?   70
What hands are here? ha! they pluck out mine eyes!
Will all great Neptune's ocean wash this blood
Clean from my hand? No; this my hand will rather
The multitudinous seas incarnadine,
Making the green one red.   75

    Reenter Lady Macbeth.

Lady Macbeth

My hands are of your color, but I shame
To wear a heart so white.

                        [*Knocking within.*
                I hear a knocking
At the south entry: retire we to our chamber:
A little water clears us of this deed: 80
How easy is it then! Your constancy
Hath left you unattended.

                        [*Knocking within.*
                Hark! more knocking:
Get on your nightgown, lest occasion call us
And show us to be watchers: be not lost   85
So poorly in your thoughts.

Macbeth

To know my deed, 'twere best not know myself.
                        [*Knocking within.*
Wake Duncan with thy knocking! I would thou
    couldst!

                        [*Exeunt.*

2 **should have old turning the key** should be extremely busy opening and closing the gate.

4 **Beelzebub** a devil.

5 **on th' expectation of plenty** The farmer killed himself because a surplus of crops caused the price to go down, when he had been holding back his produce in the hope of high prices.

8 **equivocator** reference to Jesuit priests, said to be prone to ambiguous statements; the Jesuits had been held by many to be plotters and traitors in Queen Elizabeth's time.

13–14 **English tailor** a dishonest tailor might cheat on cloth in making French hose — a skimpy style of breeches.

15 **goose** tailor's pressing iron.

21 **remember the porter** He holds out his hand for a tip as he opens the gate.

Scene 3. *The same*

Enter a Porter. Knocking within.

Porter
Here's a knocking indeed! If a man were porter of hell-
gate, he should have old turning the key. [*Knocking
within.*] Knock, knock, knock! Who's there, i' the
name of Beelzebub? Here's a farmer, that hanged
himself on th' expectation of plenty: come in time; 5
have napkins enow about you; here you'll sweat for
't. [*Knocking within.*] Knock, knock! Who's there,
in th' other devil's name? Faith, here's an equivocator, that could swear in both the scales against
either scale; who committed treason enough for 10
God's sake, yet could not equivocate to heaven:
O, come in, equivocator. [*Knocking within.*] Knock,
knock, knock! Who's there? Faith, here's an English
tailor come hither, for stealing out of a French hose:
come in, tailor; here you may roast your goose. 15
[*Knocking within.*] Knock, knock; never at quiet!
What are you? But this place is too cold for hell.
I'll devil-porter it no further: I had thought to have
let in some of all professions, that go the primrose
way to the everlasting bonfire. [*Knocking within.*] 20
Anon, anon! I pray you, remember the porter.
[*Opens the gate.*

Enter Macduff and Lennox.

Macduff
Was it so late, friend, ere you went to bed,
That you do lie so late?
Porter
Faith, sir, we were carousing till the second cock:
and drink, sir, is a great provoker of three things. 25

27 **nose-painting**   red noses.

38–40 **The porter speaks as though he wrestled with drink and won out.**

Macduff
What three things does drink especially provoke?

Porter
Marry, sir, nose-painting, sleep, and urine. Lechery,
sir, it provokes and unprovokes; it provokes the desire, but it takes away the performance: therefore
much drink may be said to be an equivocator with   30
lechery: it makes him and it mars him; it sets him
on and it takes him off; it persuades him and dis-
heartens him; makes him stand to and not stand
to; in conclusion, equivocates him in a sleep, and
giving him the lie, leaves him.   35

Macduff
I believe drink gave thee the lie last night.

Porter
That it did, sir, i' the very throat on me: but I re-
quited him for his lie, and, I think, being too strong
for him, though he took up my leg sometime, yet
I made a shift to cast him.   40

Macduff
Is thy master stirring?

   Enter Macbeth.

Our knocking has awak'd him; here he comes.

Lennox
Good morrow, noble sir.

Macbeth
                  Good morrow, both.

Macduff
Is the king stirring, worthy thane?   45

Macbeth
                       Not yet.

Macduff
He did command me to call timely on him:
I had almost slipp'd the hour.

52 physics relieves.

63 **the obscure bird** the night owl.

Macbeth

I'll bring you to him.

Macduff

I know this is a joyful trouble to you;   50
But yet 'tis one.

Macbeth

The labor we delight in physics pain.
This is the door.

Macduff

I'll make so bold to call,
For 'tis my limited service.   55

[*Exit.*

Lennox

Goes the king hence today?

Macbeth

He does: he did appoint so.

Lennox

The night has been unruly: where we lay,
Our chimneys were blown down, and, as they say,
Lamentings heard i' th' air, strange screams of death,   60
And prophesying with accents terrible
Of dire combustion and confus'd events
New hatch'd to the woeful time: the obscure bird
Clamor'd the livelong night: some say, the earth
Was feverous and did shake.   65

Macbeth

'Twas a rough night.

Lennox

My young remembrance cannot parallel
A fellow to it.

Reenter Macduff.

Macduff

O horror, horror, horror! Tongue nor heart
Cannot conceive nor name thee.   70

72 **Confusion** destruction.

74 **The Lord's anointed temple** the sacred body of the king.

79 **Gorgon** a reference to Medusa; those who looked on her were turned to stone.

87 **sprites** spirits rising from the grave.

Macbeth and Lennox

What's the matter?

Macduff

Confusion now hath made his masterpiece.
Most sacrilegious murder hath broke ope
The Lord's anointed temple, and stole thence
The life o' the building.   75

Macbeth

What is 't you say? the life?

Lennox

Mean you his majesty?

Macduff

Approach the chamber, and destroy your sight
With a new Gorgon: do not bid me speak;
See, and then speak yourselves.   80

                    [*Exeunt Macbeth and Lennox.*
                    Awake, awake!

Ring the alarum-bell. Murder and treason!
Banquo and Donalbain! Malcolm! awake!
Shake off this downy sleep, death's counterfeit,
And look on death itself! up, up, and see   85
The great doom's image! Malcolm! Banquo!
As from your graves rise up, and walk like sprites,
To countenance this horror. Ring the bell.

                                        [*Bell rings.*

   Enter Lady Macbeth.

Lady Macbeth

What's the business,
That such a hideous trumpet calls to parley   90
The sleepers of the house? speak, speak!

Macduff

                              O gentle lady,
'Tis not for you to hear what I can speak:
The repetition, in a woman's ear,
Would murder as it fell.   95

107–108 The best part of life is gone, and only the dregs are left.

Enter Banquo.

                      O Banquo, Banquo!
Our royal master's murder'd.

Lady Macbeth
                         Woe, alas!
What, in our house?

Banquo
                     Too cruel anywhere.   100
Dear Duff, I prithee, contradict thyself,
And say it is not so.

    Reenter Macbeth and Lennox, with Ross.

Macbeth
Had I but died an hour before this chance,
I had liv'd a blessed time; for from this instant
There's nothing serious in mortality: 105
All is but toys: renown and grace is dead;
The wine of life is drawn, and the mere lees
Is left this vault to brag of.

    Enter Malcolm and Donalbain.

Donalbain
What is amiss?

Macbeth
                 You are, and do not know 't: 110
The spring, the head, the fountain of your blood
Is stopp'd; the very source of it is stopp'd.

Macduff
Your royal father's murder'd.

Malcolm
                    O, by whom?

Lennox
Those of his chamber, as it seem'd, had done 't: 115
Their hands and faces were all badg'd with blood;
So were their daggers, which unwip'd we found

126 **expedition** speed, haste.

132 **breech'd** covered.

140 **an auger-hole** some unsuspected hiding place.

Upon their pillows:
They star'd, and were distracted; no man's life
Was to be trusted with them.　　　　　　　　　120

Macbeth

O, yet I do repent me of my fury,
That I did kill them.

Macduff
　　　　　　　　Wherefore did you so?

Macbeth

Who can be wise, amaz'd, temp'rate and furious,
Loyal and neutral, in a moment? No man:　　　125
The expedition of my violent love
Outrun the pauser, reason. Here lay Duncan,
His silver skin lac'd with his golden blood,
And his gash'd stabs look'd like a breach in nature
For ruin's wasteful entrance: there, the murderers,　130
Steep'd in the colors of their trade, their daggers
Unmannerly breech'd with gore: who could refrain,
That had a heart to love, and in that heart
Courage to make 's love known?

Lady Macbeth
　　　　　　　　Help me hence, ho!　　135

Macduff
Look to the lady.

Malcolm
　　[*Aside to Donalbain*]
　　　　　　　Why do we hold our tongues,
That most may claim this argument for ours?

Donalbain
　　[*Aside to Malcolm*]
What should be spoken here, where our fate,
Hid in an auger-hole, may rush, and seize us?　　140
Let's away;
Our tears are not yet brew'd.

146 our naked frailties hid   clothed our bodies.

Malcolm
   [*Aside to Donalbain*] Nor our strong sorrow
  Upon the foot of motion.

Banquo
               Look to the lady: 145
         [*Lady Macbeth is carried out.*
  And when we have our naked frailties hid,
  That suffer in exposure, let us meet,
  And question this most bloody piece of work,
  To know it further. Fears and scruples shake us:
  In the great hand of God I stand, and thence 150
  Against the undivulg'd pretense I fight
  Of treasonous malice.

Macduff
         And so do I.

All
         So all.

Macbeth
  Let's briefly put on manly readiness, 155
  And meet i' the hall together.

All
        Well contented.
    [*Exeunt all but Malcolm and Donalbain.*

Malcolm
  What will you do? Let's not consort with them:
  To show an unfelt sorrow is an office
  Which the false man does easy. I'll to England. 160

Donalbain
  To Ireland, I; our separated fortune
  Shall keep us both the safer: where we are
  There's daggers in men's smiles: the near in blood,
  The nearer bloody.

Malcolm
       This murderous shaft that's shot 165
  Hath not yet lighted, and our safest way

169–170 **there's warrant . . .** It is proper to steal when what one steals is himself, in the face of merciless danger.

8 **the traveling lamp** the sun.

15 **mousing owl** an owl that preys on mice.

Is to avoid the aim. Therefore to horse;
And let us not be dainty of leave-taking,
But shift away: there's warrant in that theft
Which steals itself when there's no mercy left.　　　170

　　　　　　　　　　　　　　　[*Exeunt.*

　　　Scene 4. Outside Macbeth's castle

　　Enter Ross with an old Man.

Old Man
　　Threescore and ten I can remember well:
　　Within the volume of which time I have seen
　　Hours dreadful and things strange, but this sore night
　　Hath trifled former knowings.

Ross
　　　　　　　　　　　　Ah, good father,　　　5
　　Thou seest the heavens, as troubled with man's act,
　　Threaten his bloody stage: by the clock 'tis day,
　　And yet dark night strangles the traveling lamp:
　　Is 't night's predominance, or the day's shame,
　　That darkness does the face of earth entomb,　　　10
　　When living light should kiss it?

Old Man
　　　　　　　　　　　　'Tis unnatural,
　　Even like the deed that's done. On Tuesday last
　　A falcon tow'ring in her pride of place
　　Was by a mousing owl hawk'd at and kill'd.　　　15

Ross
　　And Duncan's horses—a thing most strange and
　　　　　certain—
　　Beauteous and swift, the minions of their race,
　　Turn'd wild in nature, broke their stalls, flung out,

30 **pretend** have in mind, hope for.

31 **suborn'd** bribed.

36 **ravin up** devour ravenously.

39 **Scone** the place where the kings of Scotland were tradi-
   tionally crowned.
40 **invested** crowned.

Contending 'gainst obedience, as they would make
War with mankind.   20

Old Man

'Tis said they eat each other.

Ross

They did so, to th' amazement of mine eyes,
That look'd upon 't.

Enter Macduff.

Here comes the good Macduff.
How goes the world, sir, now?   25

Macduff

Why, see you not?

Ross

Is 't known who did this more than bloody deed?

Macduff

Those that Macbeth hath slain.

Ross

Alas, the day!
What good could they pretend?   30

Macduff

They were suborn'd:
Malcolm and Donalbain, the king's two sons,
Are stol'n away and fled, which puts upon them
Suspicion of the deed.

Ross

'Gainst nature still: 35
Thriftless ambition, that wilt ravin up
Thine own life's means! Then 'tis most like
The sovereignty will fall upon Macbeth.

Macduff

He is already nam'd, and gone to Scone
To be invested.   40

Ross

Where is Duncan's body?

46 Fife Macduff's own castle.

Macduff
    Carried to Colme-kill,
    The sacred storehouse of his predecessors
    And guardian of their bones.

Ross
                      Will you to Scone?   45

Macduff
    No, cousin, I'll to Fife.

Ross
                Well, I will thither.

Macduff
    Well, may you see things well done there: adieu!
    Lest our old robes sit easier than our new!

Ross
    Farewell, father.   50

Old Man
    God's benison go with you, and with those
    That would make good of bad and friends of foes!
                                [*Exeunt.*

ACT III

Scene 1. Forres. The palace

Enter Banquo.

Banquo
    Thou hast it now: king, Cawdor, Glamis, all,
    As the weird women promis'd, and I fear
    Thou play'dst most foully for 't: yet it was said
    It should not stand in thy posterity,
    But that myself should be the root and father   5

14 all-thing   altogether.

Of many kings. If there come truth from them—
As upon thee, Macbeth, their speeches shine—
Why, by the verities on thee made good,
May they not be my oracles as well
And set me up in hope? But hush, no more.   10

    Sennet sounded. Enter Macbeth, as king; Lady
    Macbeth, as queen; Lennox, Ross, Lords, Ladies,
    and Attendants.

Macbeth
Here's our chief guest.

Lady Macbeth
                If he had been forgotten,
It had been as a gap in our great feast,
And all-thing unbecoming.

Macbeth
Tonight we hold a solemn supper, sir,   15
And I'll request your presence.

Banquo
                    Let your highness
Command upon me, to the which my duties
Are with a most indissoluble tie
For ever knit.   20

Macbeth
Ride you this afternoon?

Banquo
Aye, my good lord.

Macbeth
We should have else desir'd your good advice,
Which still hath been both grave and prosperous,
In this day's council; but we'll take tomorrow.   25
Is 't far you ride?

Banquo
As far, my lord, as will fill up the time
'Twixt this and supper: go not my horse the better,

35   **parricide**   murder of a parent.

37   **cause of state**   government business.
38   **Craving us jointly**   requiring the attention of both of us.

I must become a borrower of the night
For a dark hour or twain.   30

Macbeth
                  Fail not our feast.

Banquo
My lord, I will not.

Macbeth
We hear our bloody cousins are bestow'd
In England and in Ireland, not confessing
Their cruel parricide, filling their hearers   35
With strange invention: but of that tomorrow,
When therewithal we shall have cause of state
Craving us jointly. Hie you to horse: adieu,
Till you return at night. Goes Fleance with you?

Banquo
Aye, my good lord: our time does call upon 's.   40

Macbeth
I wish your horses swift and sure of foot,
And so I do commend you to their backs.
Farewell.
                    [*Exit Banquo.*
Let every man be master of his time
Till seven at night; to make society   45
The sweeter welcome, we will keep ourself
Till supper-time alone: while then, God be with you!
        [*Exeunt all but Macbeth and an Attendant.*
Sirrah, a word with you: attend those men
Our pleasure?

Attendant
They are, my lord, without the palace gate.   50

Macbeth
Bring them before us.
                    [*Exit Attendant.*
            To be thus is nothing;
But to be safely thus: our fears in Banquo
Stick deep; and in his royalty of nature

60 **Genius** guardian spirit.
rebuk'd shamed, lowered in value.

61 **Mark Antony's was by Caesar** Augustus Caesar triumphed over Mark Antony in their struggle for power.

67 **unlineal hand** one not descended from Macbeth.

69 **fil'd** defiled.

72 **eternal jewel** the soul.
73 **the common enemy of man** Satan.

75–76 **come, fate . .** Macbeth challenges Fate to a mortal combat.

85 **pass'd in probation** examined and offered proof.

Reigns that which would be fear'd: 'tis much he dares,   55
And, to that dauntless temper of his mind,
He hath a wisdom that doth guide his valor
To act in safety. There is none but he
Whose being I do fear: and under him
My Genius is rebuk'd, as it is said   60
Mark Antony's was by Cæsar. He chid the sisters,
When first they put the name of king upon me,
And bade them speak to him; then prophet-like
They hail'd him father to a line of kings:
Upon my head they plac'd a fruitless crown   65
And put a barren scepter in my gripe,
Thence to be wrench'd with an unlineal hand,
No son of mine succeeding. If 't be so,
For Banquo's issue have I fil'd my mind;
For them the gracious Duncan have I murder'd;   70
Put rancors in the vessel of my peace
Only for them, and mine eternal jewel
Given to the common enemy of man,
To make them kings, the seed of Banquo kings!
Rather than so, come, fate, into the list,   75
And champion me to th' utterance! Who's there?

Reenter Attendant, with two Murderers.

Now go to the door, and stay there till we call.
                                        [*Exit Attendant.*
Was it not yesterday we spoke together?

First Murderer

It was, so please your highness.

Macbeth

                                Well then, now   80
Have you consider'd of my speeches? Know
That it was he in the times past which held you
So under fortune, which you thought had been
Our innocent self: this I made good to you
In our last conference; pass'd in probation with you,   85

86 **borne in hand** deceived through treachery.
cross'd thwarted.

88 **To half a soul and to a notion craz'd** even to a half-witted
or crazed understanding.

101 **Shoughs, water-rugs** types of shaggy dogs.
clept called.
102 **the valued file** the discriminating list.

107 **Particular addition** a special title to distinguish his quality
from the indiscriminate masses.

How you were borne in hand, how cross'd, the in-
    struments,
Who wrought with them, and all things else that
    might
To half a soul and to a notion craz'd
Say "Thus did Banquo."

First Murderer

                      You made it known to us.   90

Macbeth

I did so; and went further, which is now
Our point of second meeting. Do you find
Your patience so predominant in your nature,
That you can let this go? Are you so gospell'd,
To pray for this good man and for his issue,   95
Whose heavy hand hath bow'd you to the grave
And beggar'd yours for ever?

First Murderer

                   We are men, my liege.

Macbeth

Aye, in the catalogue ye go for men;
As hounds and greyhounds, mongrels, spaniels, curs,   100
Shoughs, water-rugs and demi-wolves, are clept
All by the name of dogs: the valued file
Distinguishes the swift, the slow, the subtle,
The housekeeper, the hunter, every one
According to the gift which bounteous nature   105
Hath in him clos'd, whereby he does receive
Particular addition, from the bill
That writes them all alike: and so of men.
Now if you have a station in the file,
Not i' the worst rank of manhood, say 't,   110
And I will put that business in your bosoms
Whose execution takes your enemy off,
Grapples you to the heart and love of us,
Who wear our health but sickly in his life,
Which in his death were perfect.   115

127 **bloody distance** strong enmity.

129 **near'st of life** most vital spot — the heart.

133 **but wail his fall** *Must* is understood before wail; Macbeth must appear to mourn the death of his victim Banquo.

Second Murderer

I am one, my liege,

Whom the vile blows and buffets of the world
Have so incens'd that I am reckless what
I do to spite the world.

First Murderer

And I another   120

So weary with disasters, tugg'd with fortune,
That I would set my life on any chance,
To mend it or be rid on 't.

Macbeth

Both of you

Know Banquo was your enemy.   125

Both Murderers

True, my lord.

Macbeth

So is he mine, and in such bloody distance
That every minute of his being thrusts
Against my near'st of life: and though I could
With barefac'd power sweep him from my sight   130
And bid my will avouch it, yet I must not,
For certain friends that are both his and mine,
Whose loves I may not drop, but wail his fall
Who I myself struck down: and thence it is
That I to your assistance do make love,   135
Masking the business from the common eye
For sundry weighty reasons.

Second Murderer

We shall, my lord,

Perform what you command us.

First Murderer

Though our lives—   140

Macbeth

Your spirits shine through you. Within this hour at
     most
I will advise you where to plant yourselves,

143 **Acquaint you** ... let you know exactly when the deed should be done Probably the third murderer had the responsibility. (See Scene 3.)

145 **always thought** always keeping in mind.

146 **clearness** no risk of being suspected.

Acquaint you with the perfect spy o' the time,
The moment on 't; for 't must be done tonight,
And something from the palace; always thought   145
That I require a clearness: and with him—
To leave no rubs nor botches in the work—
Fleance his son, that keeps him company,
Whose absence is no less material to me
Than is his father's, must embrace the fate   150
Of that dark hour. Resolve yourselves apart:
I'll come to you anon.

Both Murderers
           We are resolv'd, my lord.

Macbeth
I'll call upon you straight: abide within.
                  [Exeunt Murderers.
It is concluded: Banquo, thy soul's flight,   155
If it find heaven, must find it out tonight.
                        [Exit.

Scene 2. The palace

Enter Lady Macbeth and a Servant.

Lady Macbeth
Is Banquo gone from court?

Servant
Aye, madam, but returns again tonight.

Lady Macbeth
Say to the king, I would attend his leisure
For a few words.

Servant
          Madam, I will.   5
                    [Exit.

6 **spent**   used up; come to an end.

11 **sorriest**   wretched, miserable.

15 **scotch'd**   wounded.
16 **close**   come together.

18 **let the frame of things disjoint**   Let the structure of the world break up.

24 **ecstasy**   frenzy.

30 **sleek o'er**   smooth over.

34 **Present him eminence**   do him honor.

Lady Macbeth

                              Naught's had, all's spent,
Where our desire is got without content:
'Tis safer to be that which we destroy
Than by destruction dwell in doubtful joy.

Enter Macbeth.

How now, my lord! why do you keep alone,   10
Of sorriest fancies your companions making;
Using those thoughts which should indeed have died
With them they think on? Things without all remedy
Should be without regard: what's done is done.

Macbeth

We have scotch'd the snake, not kill'd it: 15
She'll close and be herself, whilst our poor malice
Remains in danger of her former tooth.
But let the frame of things disjoint, both the worlds
        suffer,
Ere we will eat our meal in fear, and sleep
In the affliction of these terrible dreams   20
That shake us nightly: better be with the dead,
Whom we, to gain our peace, have sent to peace,
Than on the torture of the mind to lie
In restless ecstasy. Duncan is in his grave;
After life's fitful fever he sleeps well;   25
Treason has done his worst: nor steel, nor poison,
Malice domestic, foreign levy, nothing,
Can touch him further.

Lady Macbeth

                        Come on;
Gentle my lord, sleek o'er your rugged looks;   30
Be bright and jovial among your guests tonight.

Macbeth

So shall I, love; and so, I pray, be you:
Let your remembrance apply to Banquo;
Present him eminence, both with eye and tongue:

35–36 The need to flatter Banquo shows how unsafe are Macbeth and Lady Macbeth.

37 **visards** masks.

42 **nature's copy's not eterne** They will not live forever.

51 **seeling** a reference to the blinding of a falcon by sewing its eyelids with silk while training it.

52 **Scarf up** cover up.

54 **that great bond** the prophecy the witches made to Banquo.

Unsafe the while, that we   35
Must lave our honors in thèse flattering streams,
And make our faces visards to our hearts,
Disguising what they are.

Lady Macbeth
                    You must leave this.

Macbeth
O, full of scorpions is my mind, dear wife!   40
Thou know'st that Banquo, and his Fleance, lives.

Lady Macbeth
But in them nature's copy's not eterne.

Macbeth
There's comfort yet; they are assailable;
Then be thou jocund: ere the bat hath flown
His cloister'd flight; ere to black Hecate's summons   45
The shard-borne beetle with his drowsy hums
Hath rung night's yawning peal, there shall be done
A deed of dreadful note.

Lady Macbeth
                    What's to be done?

Macbeth
Be innocent of the knowledge, dearest chuck,   50
Till thou applaud the deed. Come, seeling night,
Scarf up the tender eye of pitiful day,
And with thy bloody and invisible hand
Cancel and tear to pieces that great bond
Which keeps me pale! Light thickens, and the crow   55
Makes wing to the rooky wood:
Good things of day begin to droop and drowse,
Whiles night's black agents to their preys do rouse.
Thou marvel'st at my words: but hold thee still;
Things bad begun make strong themselves by ill: 60
So, prithee, go with me.

                              [*Exeunt.*

14 note of expectation   the list of expected guests

Scene 3. A park near the palace

Enter three Murderers.

First Murderer
But who did bid thee join with us?

Third Murderer

                              Macbeth.

Second Murderer
He needs not our mistrust; since he delivers
Our offices, and what we have to do,
To the direction just.   5

First Murderer
                  Then stand with us.
The west yet glimmers with some streaks of day:
Now spurs the lated traveler apace
To gain the timely inn, and near approaches
The subject of our watch.   10

Third Murderer
                  Hark! I hear horses.

Banquo
[*Within*]   Give us a light there, ho!

Second Murderer
                  Then 'tis he: the rest
That are within the note of expectation
Already are i' the court.   15

First Murderer
                  His horses go about.

Third Murderer
Almost a mile: but he does usually—
So all men do—from hence to the palace gate
Make it their walk.

Second Murderer
                  A light, a light!   20

30–31 We have failed to accomplish half of what we were to do.

Enter Banquo, and Fleance with a torch.

Third Murderer

'Tis he.

First Murderer
Stand to 't.
Banquo
It will be rain tonight.
First Murderer

Let it come down.
[They set upon Banquo.

Banquo
O, treachery! Fly, good Fleance, fly, fly, fly!   25
Thou mayst revenge. O slave!
[Dies. Fleance escapes.

Third Murderer
Who did strike out the light?
First Murderer

Was 't not the way?

Third Murderer
There's but one down; the son is fled.
Second Murderer

We have lost   30
Best half of our affair.
First Murderer
Well, let's away and say how much is done.
[Exeunt.

1 **degrees** rank; the guests are seated according to rank.

6 **keeps her state** remains seated on her throne, apart from the table where the guests sit.

11 **Both sides are even** The seats at both sides of the table are occupied; Macbeth plans to sit at the head of the table.

Scene 4. Hall in the palace

*A banquet prepared. Enter Macbeth, Lady Macbeth,
Ross, Lennox, Lords, and Attendants.*

Macbeth

You know your own degrees; sit down: at first
And last a hearty welcome.

Lords

                    Thanks to your majesty.

Macbeth

Ourself will mingle with society
And play the humble host.   5
Our hostess keeps her state, but in best time
We will require her welcome.

Lady Macbeth

Pronounce it for me, sir, to all our friends,
For my heart speaks they are welcome.

   Enter first Murderer to the door.

Macbeth

See, they encounter thee with their hearts' thanks.   10
Both sides are even: here I'll sit i' the midst:
Be large in mirth; anon we'll drink a measure
The table round.

                   [Approaching the door.
       There's blood upon thy face.

Murderer

'Tis Banquo's then.   15

Macbeth

'Tis better thee without than he within.
Is he dispatch'd?

Murderer

My lord, his throat is cut; that I did for him.

26 **As broad and general** . . . as free as the air that surrounds us.

38 **give the cheer** make your guests feel welcome.

38–42 **the feast is sold** . . . The host must be welcoming and hospitable if a feast is to be a genuine occasion; otherwise, it had might as well be a meal that is purchased, or eaten at home.

43 **remembrancer** one who reminds him of his obligation.

Macbeth

Thou art the best o' the cutthroats: yet he's good
That did the like for Fleance: if thou didst it,   20
Thou art the nonpareil.

Murderer

                              Most royal sir,
Fleance is 'scap'd.

Macbeth

   [*Aside*]
Then comes my fit again: I had else been perfect,
Whole as the marble, founded as the rock,   25
As broad and general as the casing air:
But now I am cabin'd, cribb'd, confin'd, bound in
To saucy doubts and fears.—But Banquo's safe?

Murderer

Aye, my good lord: safe in a ditch he bides,
With twenty trenched gashes on his head;   30
The least a death to nature.

Macbeth

                              Thanks for that.
   [*Aside*]
There the grown serpent lies; the worm that's fled
Hath nature that in time will venom breed,
No teeth for the present. Get thee gone: tomorrow   35
We'll hear ourselves again.

                              [*Exit Murderer.*

Lady Macbeth

                         My royal lord,
You do not give the cheer: the feast is sold
That is not often vouch'd, while 'tis a making,
'Tis given with welcome: to feed were best at home;   40
From thence the sauce to meat is ceremony;
Meeting were bare without it.

Macbeth

                         Sweet remembrancer!

47–48 As these words are spoken, Macbeth has not yet seen the ghost of Banquo sitting in Macbeth's place.

49–50 Macbeth is inclined to blame Banquo for unkindness in not coming, rather than pity him for some accident that may have befallen him.

54 All the seats seem occupied; Macbeth does not yet distinguish Banquo's ghost.

Now good digestion wait on appetite,

And health on both!   45
Lennox

     May 't please your highness sit.

The Ghost of Banquo enters, and sits in Macbeth's place.

Macbeth

Here had we now our country's honor roof'd,
Were the grac'd person of our Banquo present;
Who may I rather challenge for unkindness
Than pity for mischance!   50

Ross

     His absence, sir,
Lays blame upon his promise. Please 't your highness
To grace us with your royal company.

Macbeth

The table's full.

Lennox

    Here is a place reserv'd, sir.   55

Macbeth

Where?

Lennox

Here, my good lord. What is 't that moves your
  highness?

Macbeth

Which of you have done this?

Lords

     What, my good lord?

Macbeth

Thou canst not say I did it: never shake   60
Thy gory locks at me.

Ross

Gentlemen, rise; his highness is not well.

68 **Are you a man?** spoken privately to Macbeth. These words and those that follow are not heard by the guests.

75 **Imposters to true fears** tricks of the imagination, not genuine fears.

80–84 As these words are spoken, the ghost rises, nods his head, and moves offstage.

82 **charnel-houses** storehouses for corpses.

84 **the maws of kites** The only monuments for the dead shall be the bellies of the birds (kites) that devour them.

Lady Macbeth

Sit, worthy friends: my lord is often thus,
And hath been from his youth: pray you, keep seat;
The fit is momentary; upon a thought   65
He will again be well: if much you note him,
You shall offend him and extend his passion:
Feed, and regard him not. Are you a man?

Macbeth

Aye, and a bold one, that dare look on that
Which might appal the devil.   70

Lady Macbeth

                    O proper stuff!
This is the very painting of your fear:
This is the air-drawn dagger which, you said,
Led you to Duncan. O, these flaws and starts,
Impostors to true fear, would well become   75
A woman's story at a winter's fire,
Authoriz'd by her grandam. Shame itself!
Why do you make such faces? When all's done,
You look but on a stool.

Macbeth

Prithee, see there! behold! look! lo! how say you?   80
Why, what care I? If thou canst nod, speak too.
If charnel-houses and our graves must send
Those that we bury back, our monuments
Shall be the maws of kites.

                                        [*Exit Ghost.*

Lady Macbeth

                    What, quite unmann'd in folly?   85

Macbeth

If I stand here, I saw him.

Lady Macbeth

                    Fie, for shame!

Macbeth

Blood hath been shed ere now, i' th' olden time,

89 **Ere humane statute ...** before humane laws cleansed society of violence and civilized it.

105 The ghost reenters as Macbeth proposes this toast.

111 **speculation** genuine ability to see.

Ere humane statute purg'd the gentle weal;
Aye, and since too, murders have been perform'd   90
Too terrible for the ear: the time has been,
That, when the brains were out, the man would die,
And there an end; but now they rise again,
With twenty mortal murders on their crowns,
And push us from our stools: this is more strange   95
Than such a murder is.

Lady Macbeth
                    My worthy lord,
Your noble friends do lack you.

Macbeth
                         I do forget.
Do not muse at me, my most worthy friends;   100
I have a strange infirmity, which is nothing
To those that know me. Come, love and health to all;
Then I'll sit down. Give me some wine, fill full.
I drink to the general joy o' the whole table,
And to our dear friend Banquo, whom we miss;   105
Would he were here! to all and him we thirst,
And all to all.

Lords
          Our duties, and the pledge.

          Reenter Ghost.

Macbeth
Avaunt! and quit my sight! let the earth hide thee!
Thy bones are marrowless, thy blood is cold;   110
Thou hast no speculation in those eyes
Which thou dost glare with.

Lady Macbeth
                    Think of this, good peers,
But as a thing of custom: 'tis no other;
Only it spoils the pleasure of the time.   115

Macbeth
What man dare, I dare:

118 **Hyrcan tiger** a reference to fierce tigers in the area of ancient Hyrcania.

128 **admir'd** amazing, wondered at.

131–132 **You make me strange . . .** You make me feel I am ignorant of my own character or nature.

135 **blanch'd** whitened.

Approach thou like the rugged Russian bear,
The arm'd rhinoceros, or the Hyrcan tiger;
Take any shape but that, and my firm nerves
Shall never tremble: or be alive again,   120
And dare me to the desert with thy sword;
If trembling I inhabit then, protest me
The baby of a girl. Hence, horrible shadow!
Unreal mockery, hence!
                            [*Exit Ghost.*
                        Why, so: being gone,   125
I am a man again. Pray you. sit still.

Lady Macbeth

You have displac'd the mirth, broke the good meeting,
With most admir'd disorder.

Macbeth

                        Can such things be,
And overcome us like a summer's cloud,   130
Without our special wonder? You make me strange
Even to the disposition that I owe,
When now I think you can behold such sights,
And keep the natural ruby of your cheeks,
When mine is blanch'd with fear.   135

Ross

                        What sights, my lord?

Lady Macbeth

I pray you, speak not; he grows worse and worse;
Question enrages him: at once, good night:
Stand not upon the order of your going,
But go at once.   140

Lennox

                Good night; and better health
Attend his majesty!

Lady Macbeth

                A kind good night to all!
            [*Exeunt all but Macbeth and Lady Macbeth.*

145 Macbeth is giving instances of unnatural events which re-
sulted in the revelation of murders.

146 **Augures and understood relations** predictions and inter-
pretations. The reference is to the alleged power of birds
(maggot-pies, etc.) to offer predictions and comprehension
of events to those skilled in interpretation.

148 **secret'st man of blood** the most secret murderer.

164 **season** that which preserves.

165 **self-abuse** self-deception.

Macbeth

It will have blood: they say blood will have blood:
Stones have been known to move and trees to speak; 145
Augures and understood relations have
By maggot-pies and choughs and rooks brought forth
The secret'st man of blood. What is the night?

Lady Macbeth

Almost at odds with morning, which is which.

Macbeth

How say'st thou, that Macduff denies his person 150
At our great bidding?

Lady Macbeth

              Did you send to him, sir?

Macbeth

I hear it by the way, but I will send:
There's not a one of them but in his house
I keep a servant fee'd. I will tomorrow, 155
And betimes I will, to the weird sisters:
More shall they speak, for now I am bent to know,
By the worst means, the worst. For mine own good
All causes shall give way: I am in blood
Stepp'd in so far that, should I wade no more, 160
Returning were as tedious as go o'er:
Strange things I have in head that will to hand,
Which must be acted ere they may be scann'd.

Lady Macbeth

You lack the season of all natures, sleep.

Macbeth

Come, we'll to sleep. My strange and self-abuse 165
Is the initiate fear that wants hard use:
We are yet but young in deed.

                         [*Exeunt.*

2 **beldams** hags.

15 **Acheron** a river in Hades.

29 **confusion** destruction.

Scene 5. A heath

Thunder. Enter the three Witches, meeting Hecate.

First Witch
   Why, how now, Hecate! you look angerly.
Hecate
   Have I not reason, beldams as you are,
   Saucy and overbold? How did you dare
   To trade and traffic with Macbeth
   In riddles and affairs of death;   5
   And I, the mistress of your charms,
   The close contriver of all harms,
   Was never call'd to bear my part,
   Or show the glory of our art?
   And, which is worse, all you have done   10
   Hath been but for a wayward son,
   Spiteful and wrathful; who, as others do,
   Loves for his own ends, not for you.
   But make amends now: get you gone,
   And at the pit of Acheron   15
   Meet me i' the morning: thither he
   Will come to know his destiny:
   Your vessels and your spells provide,
   Your charms and every thing beside.
   I am for th' air; this night I'll spend   20
   Unto a dismal and a fatal end:
   Great business must be wrought ere noon:
   Upon the corner of the moon
   There hangs a vap'rous drop profound;
   I'll catch it ere it comes to ground: 25
   And that distill'd by magic sleights
   Shall raise such artificial sprights
   As by the strength of their illusion
   Shall draw him on to his confusion:

8 **cannot want** can avoid.

He shall spurn fate, scorn death, and bear   30
His hopes 'bove wisdom, grace and fear:
And you all know security
Is mortals' chiefest enemy.

> [*Music and a song within:* "*Come
> away, come away,*" *&c.*

Hark! I am call'd; my little spirit, see,
Sits in a foggy cloud, and stays for me.   35

> [*Exit.*

First Witch
Come, let's make haste; she'll soon be back again.

> [*Exeunt.*

Scene 6. Forres. The palace

Enter Lennox and another Lord.

Lennox
My former speeches have but hit your thoughts,
Which can interpret farther: only I say
Things have been strangely borne. The gracious
    Duncan
Was pitied of Macbeth: marry, he was dead:
And the right-valiant Banquo walk'd too late;   5
Whom, you may say, if 't please you, Fleance kill'd,
For Fleance fled: men must not walk too late.
Who cannot want the thought, how monstrous
It was for Malcolm and for Donalbain
To kill their gracious father? damned fact!   10
How it did grieve Macbeth! did he not straight,
In pious rage, the two delinquents tear,
That were the slaves of drink and thralls of sleep?
Was not that nobly done? Aye, and wisely too;
For 'twould have anger'd any heart alive   15

21 **broad words** talking too freely, without restraint.

26 **holds the due of birth** withholds his birthright.

32 **Siward** the English Earl of Northumberland.

43–45 **The cloudy messenger . . .** The messenger is unhappy that he must return to Macbeth with such an unwelcome, negative answer; he returns reluctantly.

To hear the men deny 't. So that, I say,
He has borne all things well: and I do think
That, had he Duncan's sons under his key—
As, an 't please heaven, he shall not—they should find
What 'twere to kill a father; so should Fleance.　　　20
But, peace! for from broad words, and 'cause he fail'd
His presence at the tyrant's feast, I hear,
Macduff lives in disgrace: sir, can you tell
Where he bestows himself?

Lord

　　　　　　　　　The son of Duncan,　　　25
From whom this tyrant holds the due of birth,
Lives in the English court, and is receiv'd
Of the most pious Edward with such grace
That the malevolence of fortune nothing
Takes from his high respect. Thither Macduff　　　30
Is gone to pray the holy king, upon his aid
To wake Northumberland and warlike Siward:
That by the help of these, with Him above
To ratify the work, we may again
Give to our tables meat, sleep to our nights,　　　35
Free from our feasts and banquets bloody knives,
Do faithful homage and receive free honors:
All which we pine for now: and this report
Hath so exasperate the king that he
Prepares for some attempt of war.　　　40

Lennox

　　　　　　　　　Sent he to Macduff?

Lord

He did: and with an absolute "Sir, not I,"
The cloudy messenger turns me his back,
And hums, as who should say "You'll rue the time
That clogs me with this answer."　　　45

Lennox

　　　　　　　　　And that well might
Advise him to a caution, to hold what distance

1   **brinded**   striped.

3   **Harpier**   the "familiar" of the third witch. (See note, Act I, Scene 1, lines 9, 10.)

8   **Swelter'd**   sweated.

His wisdom can provide. Some holy angel
Fly to the court of England and unfold
His message ere he come, that a swift blessing 50
May soon return to this our suffering country
Under a hand accurs'd!

Lord

I'll send my prayers with him.
[*Exeunt.*

ACT IV

Scene 1. A cavern. In the middle, a boiling cauldron

Thunder. Enter the three Witches.

First Witch
Thrice the brinded cat hath mew'd.
Second Witch
Thrice and once the hedge-pig whin'd.
Third Witch
Harpier cries " 'Tis time, 'tis time."
First Witch
Round about the cauldron go:
In the poison'd entrails throw. 5
Toad, that under cold stone
Days and nights has thirty-one
Swelter'd venom sleeping got,
Boil thou first i' the charmed pot.
All
Double, double toil and trouble; 10
Fire burn and cauldron bubble.

17 **howlet** owlet.

23 **maw and gulf** stomach and gullet.
24 **ravin'd** ravenous, voracious.

27 **slips of yew** twigs of the yew tree, supposedly poisonous.

31 **drab** harlot.
32 **slab** viscous and slimy.
33 **chaudron** intestines.

39—43 Hecate's speech is thought to have been interpolated, not part of the original play.

Second Witch
  Fillet of a fenny snake,
  In the cauldron boil and bake;
  Eye of newt and toe of frog,
  Wool of bat and tongue of dog,   15
  Adder's fork and blind-worm's sting,
  Lizard's leg and howlet's wing,
  For a charm of pow'rful trouble,
  Like a hell-broth boil and bubble.

All
  Double, double toil and trouble;   20
  Fire burn and cauldron bubble.

Third Witch
  Scale of dragon, tooth of wolf,
  Witches' mummy, maw and gulf
  Of the ravin'd salt-sea shark,
  Root of hemlock digg'd i' the dark,   25
  Liver of blaspheming Jew,
  Gall of goat and slips of yew
  Sliver'd in the moon's eclipse,
  Nose of Turk and Tartar's lips,
  Finger of birth-strangled babe   30
  Ditch-deliver'd by a drab,
  Make the gruel thick and slab:
  Add thereto a tiger's chaudron,
  For th' ingredients of our cauldron.

All
  Double, double toil and trouble;   35
  Fire burn and cauldron bubble.

Second Witch
  Cool it with a baboon's blood,
  Then the charm is firm and good.

        Enter Hecate to the other three Witches.

Hecate
  O, well done! I commend your pains;

54 **yesty** foaming (like yeast).

56 **lodg'd** beaten down.

59–60 **though the treasure ...** though all the seeds (germens) from which future growth comes should be destroyed.

And every one shall share i' the gains: 40
And now about the cauldron sing,
Like elves and fairies in a ring,
Enchanting all that you put in.
> [*Music and a song: "Black spirits," &c.*
> [*Hecate retires.*

Second Witch
By the pricking of my thumbs,
Something wicked this way comes: 45
> Open, locks,
> Whoever knocks!

    Enter Macbeth.

Macbeth
How now, you secret, black, and midnight hags!
What is 't you do?

All
> A deed without a name.   50

Macbeth
I conjure you, by that which you profess,
Howe'er you come to know it, answer me:
Though you untie the winds and let them fight
Against the churches! though the yesty waves
Confound and swallow navigation up;   55
Though bladed corn be lodg'd and trees blown down;
Though castles topple on their warders' heads;
Though palaces and pyramids do slope
Their heads to their foundations; though the treasure
Of nature's germens tumble all together,   60
Even till destruction sicken; answer me
To what I ask you.

First Witch
> Speak.

Second Witch
> Demand.

71 gibbet gallows.

81 harp'd figure of speech meaning *sounded* or *expressed*.

Third Witch

                                    We'll answer.   65

First Witch

Say, if thou'dst rather hear it from our mouths,
Or from our masters?

Macbeth

                        Call 'em, let me see 'em.

First Witch

Pour in sow's blood, that hath eaten
Her nine farrow; grease that's sweaten   70
From the murderer's gibbet throw
Into the flame.

All

                    Come, high or low;
Thyself and office deftly show!

  Thunder. First Apparition: an armed Head.

Macbeth

Tell me, thou unknown power—   75

First Witch

                            He knows thy thought:
Hear his speech, but say thou nought.

First Apparition

Macbeth! Macbeth! Macbeth! beware Macduff;
Beware the thane of Fife. Dismiss me: enough.
                                    [*Descends.*

Macbeth

Whate'er thou art, for thy good caution thanks;   80
Thou hast harp'd my fear aright: but one word more—

First Witch

He will not be commanded: here's another,
More potent than the first.

  Thunder. Second Apparition: a bloody Child.

Second Apparition

Macbeth! Macbeth! Macbeth!

105   impress   force into service.

Macbeth

　　Had I three ears, I'd hear thee.　　　　　　　　　　85

Second Apparition

　　Be bloody, bold and resolute; laugh to scorn
　　The pow'r of man, for none of woman born
　　Shall harm Macbeth.

　　　　　　　　　　　　　　　　[*Descends.*

Macbeth

　　Then live, Macduff: what need I fear of thee?
　　But yet I'll make assurance doubly sure,　　　　　90
　　And take a bond of fate: thou shalt not live;
　　That I may tell pale-hearted fear it lies,
　　And sleep in spite of thunder.

　　　　*Thunder. Third Apparition: a Child crowned, with
　　　　a tree in his hand.*

　　　　　　　　　　　　　　What is this,
　　That rises like the issue of a king,　　　　　　　95
　　And wears upon his baby-brow the round
　　And top of sovereignty?

All

　　　　　　　　　　　Listen, but speak not to 't.

Third Apparition

　　Be lion-mettled, proud, and take no care
　　Who chafes, who frets, or where conspirers are:　　100
　　Macbeth shall never vanquish'd be until
　　Great Birnam wood to high Dunsinane hill
　　Shall come against him.

　　　　　　　　　　　　　　　　[*Descends.*

Macbeth

　　　　　　　　　　That will never be:
　　Who can impress the forest, bid the tree　　　　　105
　　Unfix his earth-bound root? Sweet bodements! good!
　　Rebellion's head, rise never, till the wood
　　Of Birnam rise, and our high-plac'd Macbeth

124 **sear** scorch, burn.

132 **two-fold balls and treble scepters** symbols of sovereignty;
two-fold probably refers to England and Scotland; *treble* to
England, Scotland, and Ireland — all ruled by later English
kings.

Shall live the lease of nature, pay his breath
To time and mortal custom. Yet my heart   110
Throbs to know one thing: tell me, if your art
Can tell so much: shall Banquo's issue ever
Reign in this kingdom?

All

                    Seek to know no more.

Macbeth

I will be satisfied: deny me this,   115
And an eternal curse fall on you! Let me know:
Why sinks that cauldron? and what noise is this?
                        [*Hautboys.*

First Witch

Show!

Second Witch

Show!

Third Witch

Show!   120

All

Show his eyes, and grieve his heart;
Come like shadows, so depart!

    *A show of eight Kings, the last with a glass in his
    hand; Banquo's Ghost following.*

Macbeth

Thou art too like the spirit of Banquo: down!
Thy crown does sear mine eyeballs. And thy hair,
Thou other gold-bound brow, is like the first.   125
A third is like the former. Filthy hags!
Why do you show me this? A fourth! Start, eyes!
What, will the line stretch out to the crack of doom?
Another yet! A seventh! I'll see no more:
And yet the eighth appears, who bears a glass   130
Which shows me many more; and some I see
That two-fold balls and treble scepters carry:
Horrible sight! Now I see 'tis true;

134 blood-bolter'd his head matted with blood.

For the blood-bolter'd Banquo smiles upon me,
And points at them for his. What, is this so?   135

First Witch

Aye, sir, all this is so: but why
Stands Macbeth thus amazedly?
Come, sisters, cheer we up his sprites,
And show the best of our delights:
I'll charm the air to give a sound,   140
While you perform your antic round,
That this great king may kindly say
Our duties did his welcome pay.

       [*Music. The Witches dance, and then
                     vanish, with Hecate.*

Macbeth

Where are they? Gone? Let this pernicious hour
Stand aye accursed in the calendar!   145
Come in, without there!

    Enter Lennox.

Lennox

                    What's your grace's will?

Macbeth

Saw you the weird sisters?

Lennox

                 No, my lord.

Macbeth

Came they not by you?   150

Lennox

                No indeed, my lord.

Macbeth

Infected be the air whereon they ride,
And damn'd all those that trust them! I did hear
The galloping of horse: who was 't came by?

Lennox

'Tis two or three, my lord, that bring you word   155
Macduff is fled to England.

160 **The flighty purpose** Intentions are only fleeting; they must be immediately fulfilled.

162 **firstlings** A firstling is a first-born child — in this case, the first impulse he feels.

Macbeth

                      Fled to England!

Lennox

  Aye, my good lord.

Macbeth

  [*Aside*]   Time, thou anticipat'st my dread exploits:
  The flighty purpose never is o'ertook   160
  Unless the deed go with it: from this moment
  The very firstlings of my heart shall be
  The firstlings of my hand. And even now,
  To crown my thoughts with acts, be it thought and
      done:
  The castle of Macduff I will surprise;   165
  Seize upon Fife; give to the edge o' the sword
  His wife, his babes, and all unfortunate souls
  That trace him in his line. No boasting like a fool;
  This deed I'll do before this purpose cool:
  But no more sights!—Where are these gentlemen?   170
  Come, bring me where they are.

                               [*Exeunt.*

Scene 2. Fife. Macduff's castle

Enter Lady Macduff, her Son, and Ross.

Lady Macduff

  What had he done, to make him fly the land?

Ross

  You must have patience, madam.

Lady Macduff

                        He had none:
  His flight was madness: when our actions do not,
  Our fears do make us traitors.   5

11 **wants the natural touch** lacks natural instinct.

18 **school yourself** control yourself.

21–22 **when we are traitors ...** when we are held to be traitors but don't know what we have done that is treasonable.

22–23 **when we hold rumor ...** when our fears make us believe in rumors, yet these same fears are vague and uncertain.

Ross

                     You know not
Whether it was his wisdom or his fear.

Lady Macduff

Wisdom! to leave his wife, to leave his babes,
His mansion and his titles, in a place
From whence himself does fly? He loves us not;   10
He wants the natural touch: for the poor wren,
The most diminutive of birds, will fight,
Her young ones in her nest, against the owl.
All is the fear and nothing is the love;
As little is the wisdom, where the flight   15
So runs against all reason.

Ross

                   My dearest coz,
I pray you, school yourself: but, for your husband,
He is noble, wise, judicious, and best knows
The fits o' the season. I dare not speak much further: 20
But cruel are the times, when we are traitors
And do not know ourselves; when we hold rumor
From what we fear, yet know not what we fear,
But float upon a wild and violent sea
Each way and move. I take my leave of you: 25
Shall not be long but I'll be here again:
Things at the worst will cease, or else climb upward
To what they were before. My pretty cousin,
Blessing upon you!

Lady Macduff

Father'd he is, and yet he's fatherless.   30

Ross

I am so much a fool, should I stay longer,
It would be my disgrace and your discomfort:
I take my leave at once.

                               [*Exit.*

Lady Macduff

                   Sirrah, your father's dead:

39–40 net nor lime, / The pitfall nor the gin references to traps set for birds.

And what will you do now? How will you live?　35

Son

As birds do, mother.

Lady Macduff

　　　　　　　What, with worms and flies?

Son

With what I get, I mean; and so do they.

Lady Macduff

Poor bird! thou'dst never fear the net nor lime,

The pitfall nor the gin.　40

Son

Why should I, mother? Poor birds they are not set for.

My father is not dead, for all your saying.

Lady Macduff

Yes, he is dead: how wilt thou do for a father?

Son

Nay, how will you do for a husband?

Lady Macduff

Why, I can buy me twenty at any market.　45

Son

Then you'll buy 'em to sell again.

Lady Macduff

Thou speak'st with all thy wit, and yet, i' faith,

With wit enough for thee.

Son

Was my father a traitor, mother?

Lady Macduff

Aye, that he was.　50

Son

What is a traitor?

Lady Macduff

Why, one that swears and lies.

Son

And be all traitors that do so?

69 in your state of honor I am perfect I am fully aware of
    your honored position.

Lady Macduff
Every one that does so is a traitor, and must be
    hanged.

Son
And must they all be hanged that swear and lie?   55

Lady Macduff
Every one.

Son
Who must hang them?

Lady Macduff
Why, the honest men.

Son
Then the liars and swearers are fools; for there are
liars and swearers enow to beat the honest men and   60
hang up them.

Lady Macduff
Now, God help thee, poor monkey!
But how wilt thou do for a father?

Son
If he were dead, you'd weep for him: if you would
not, it were a good sign that I should quickly have a   65
new father.

Lady Macduff
Poor prattler, how thou talk'st!

    Enter a Messenger.

Messenger
Bless you, fair dame! I am not to you known,
Though in your state of honor I am perfect.
I doubt some danger does approach you nearly: 70
If you will take a homely man's advice,
Be not found here; hence, with your little ones.
To fright you thus, methinks I am too savage;
To do worse to you were fell cruelty,

88 shag-ear'd with long, rough hair like that of a dog.

Which is too nigh your person. Heaven preserve you!   75
I dare abide no longer.

[*Exit.*

Lady Macduff

Whither should I fly?
I have done no harm. But I remember now
I am in this earthly world, where to do harm
Is often laudable, to do good sometime   80
Accounted dangerous folly: why then, alas,
Do I put up that womanly defense,
To say I have done no harm?—What are these faces?

Enter Murderers.

First Murderer
Where is your husband?
Lady Macduff
I hope, in no place so unsanctified   85
Where such as thou mayst find him.
First Murderer

He's a traitor.

Son
Thou liest, thou shag-ear'd villain!
First Murderer

What, you egg!
[*Stabbing him.*
Young fry of treachery!   90
Son

He has kill'd me, mother:
Run away, I pray you!

[*Dies.*
[*Exit Lady Macduff, crying "Murderer!"*
Exeunt murderers, following her.

5 Bestride our downfall'n birthdom   fight for our desolated native land.

9 Like syllable of dolor   similar sounds of grief. *Like* here means *similar.*

17 wisdom   it may be wisdom for you.

22–23 recoil / In an imperial charge   yield to the demands of a king.

24 That which you are, my thoughts cannot transpose   What you really are cannot be changed by my thoughts or suspicions.

Scene 3. England. Before the King's palace

Enter Malcolm and Macduff.

Malcolm
> Let us seek out some desolate shade, and there
> Weep our sad bosoms empty.

Macduff
>   Let us rather
> Hold fast the mortal sword, and like good men
> Bestride our downfall'n birthdom: each new morn   5
> New widows howl, new orphans cry, new sorrows
> Strike heaven on the face, that it resounds
> As if it felt with Scotland and yell'd out
> Like syllable of dolor.

Malcolm
>   What I believe, I'll wail;   10
> What know, believe; and what I can redress,
> As I shall find the time to friend, I will.
> What you have spoke, it may be so perchance.
> This tyrant, whose sole name blisters our tongues,
> Was once thought honest: you have lov'd him well;   15
> He hath not touch'd you yet. I am young; but
>   something
> You may deserve of him through me; and wisdom
> To offer up a weak, poor, innocent lamb
> To appease an angry god.

Macduff
> I am not treacherous.   20

Malcolm
>   But Macbeth is.
> A good and virtuous nature may recoil
> In an imperial charge. But I shall crave your pardon;
> That which you are, my thoughts cannot transpose:
> Angels are bright still, though the brightest fell: 25

33–34 Let not my jealousies . . . Don't consider my suspicions as designed to dishonor you; they arise from a regard for my own safety.

38 wear thou thy wrongs keep what you have secured through evil.

39 The title is affeer'd Tyranny's title is legally affirmed.

49 England the king of England.

Though all things foul would wear the brows of grace,
Yet grace must still look so.

Macduff

I have lost my hopes.

Malcolm

Perchance even there where I did find my doubts.
Why in that rawness left you wife and child,   30
Those precious motives, those strong knots of love,
Without leave-taking? I pray you,
Let not my jealousies be your dishonors,
But mine own safeties. You may be rightly just,
Whatever I shall think.   35

Macduff

Bleed, bleed, poor country:
Great tyranny, lay thou thy basis sure,
For goodness dare not check thee: wear thou thy
        wrongs;
The title is affeer'd. Fare thee well, lord:
I would not be the villain that thou think'st   40
For the whole space that's in the tyrant's grasp
And the rich East to boot.

Malcolm

Be not offended:
I speak not as in absolute fear of you.
I think our country sinks beneath the yoke;   45
It weeps, it bleeds, and each new day a gash
Is added to her wounds: I think withal
There would be hands uplifted in my right;
And here from gracious England have I offer
Of goodly thousands: but for all this,   50
When I shall tread upon the tyrant's head,
Or wear it on my sword, yet my poor country
Shall have more vices than it had before,
More suffer and more sundry ways than ever,
By him that shall succeed.   55

58 the particulars of vice so grafted   the species of vice are so
    implanted.

73 continent impediments   restraints.

Macduff

           What should he be?

Malcolm

    It is myself I mean: in whom I know
    All the particulars of vice so grafted
    That, when they shall be open'd, black Macbeth
    Will seem as pure as snow, and the poor state   60
    Esteem him as a lamb, being compar'd
    With my confineless harms.

Macduff

           Not in the legions
    Of horrid hell can come a devil more damn'd
    In evils to top Macbeth.   65

Malcolm

           I grant him bloody,
    Luxurious, avaricious, false, deceitful,
    Sudden, malicious, smacking of every sin
    That has a name: but there's no bottom, none,
    In my voluptuousness: your wives, your daughters,   70
    Your matrons, and your maids, could not fill up
    The cistern of my lust, and my desire
    All continent impediments would o'erbear,
    That did oppose my will: better Macbeth
    Than such an one to reign.   75

Macduff

           Boundless intemperance
    In nature is a tyranny; it hath been
    The untimely emptying of the happy throne,
    And fall of many kings. But fear not yet
    To take upon you what is yours: you may   80
    Convey your pleasures in a spacious plenty,
    And yet seem cold, the time you may so hoodwink:
    We have willing dames enough; there cannot be
    That vulture in you, to devour so many
    As will to greatness dedicate themselves,   85
    Finding it so inclin'd.

88 affection character.
89 stanchless insatiable.

100 foisons supplies.
101 portable bearable.

Malcolm
                              With this there grows
In my most ill-compos'd affection such
A stanchless avarice that, were I king,
I should cut off the nobles for their lands,   90
Desire his jewels and this other's house:
And my more-having would be as a sauce
To make me hunger more, that I should forge
Quarrels unjust against the good and loyal,
Destroying them for wealth.   95

Macduff
                              This avarice
Sticks deeper, grows with more pernicious root
Than summer-seeming lust, and it hath been
The sword of our slain kings: yet do not fear;
Scotland hath foisons to fill up your will   100
Of your mere own: all these are portable,
With other graces weigh'd.

Malcolm
But I have none: the king-becoming graces,
As justice, verity, temp'rance, stableness,
Bounty, perseverance, mercy, lowliness,   105
Devotion, patience, courage, fortitude,
I have no relish of them, but abound
In the division of each several crime,
Acting in many ways. Nay, had I power, I should
Pour the sweet milk of concord into hell,   110
Uproar the universal peace, confound
All unity on earth.

Macduff
                    O Scotland, Scotland!

Malcolm
If such a one be fit to govern, speak:
I am as I have spoken.   115

121 interdiction a religious term implying banishment from the Church.

133 trains plots, tricks.

141 forsworn to *forswear* is to swear falsely.

Macduff

Fit to govern!
No, not to live. O nation miserable!
With an untitled tyrant bloody-scepter'd,
When shalt thou see thy wholesome days again,
Since that the truest issue of thy throne   120
By his own interdiction stands accurs'd,
And does blaspheme his breed? Thy royal father
Was a most sainted king: the queen that bore thee,
Oft'ner upon her knees than on her feet,
Died every day she liv'd. Fare thee well!   125
These evils thou repeat'st upon thyself
Have banish'd me from Scotland. O my breast,
Thy hope ends here!

Malcolm

Macduff, this noble passion,
Child of integrity, hath from my soul   130
Wip'd the black scruples, reconcil'd my thoughts
To thy good truth and honor. Devilish Macbeth
By many of these trains hath sought to win me
Into his power; and modest wisdom plucks me
From over-credulous haste: but God above   135
Deal between thee and me! for even now
I put myself to thy direction, and
Unspeak mine own detraction; here abjure
The taints and blames I laid upon myself,
For strangers to my nature. I am yet   140
Unknown to woman, never was forsworn,
Scarcely have coveted what was mine own,
At no time broke my faith, would not betray
The devil to his fellow, and delight
No less in truth than life: my first false speaking   145
Was this upon myself: what I am truly,
Is thine and my poor country's to command:
Whither indeed, before thy here-approach,
Old Siward, with ten thousand warlike men,

151–152 **the chance of goodness . . .** may our chance of success equal the justice of our cause.

157–158 **their malady convinces . . .** *convince* here means *conquer;* their illness is not susceptible to the best efforts of the medical art.

163 **the evil** scrofula (tuberculosis of lymph glands), known as the "king's evil." King Edward of England was deemed to be capable of curing this disease by a touch of his hand.

Already at a point, was setting forth.   150
Now we'll together, and the chance of goodness
Be like our warranted quarrel! Why are you silent?

Macduff

Such welcome and unwelcome things at once
'Tis hard to reconcile.

    Enter a Doctor.

Malcolm

Well, more anon. Comes the king forth, I pray you?   155

Doctor

Aye, sir; there are a crew of wretched souls
That stay his cure: their malady convinces
The great assay of art; but at his touch,
Such sanctity hath heaven given his hand,
They presently amend.   160

Malcolm

               I thank you, doctor.
                    [*Exit Doctor.*

Macduff

What's the disease he means?

Malcolm

               'Tis call'd the evil:
A most miraculous work in this good king;
Which often, since my here-remain in England,   165
I have seen him do. How he solicits heaven,
Himself best knows: but strangely-visited people,
All swol'n and ulcerous, pitiful to the eye,
The mere despair of surgery, he cures,
Hanging a golden stamp about their necks,   170
Put on with holy prayers: and 'tis spoken,
To the succeeding royalty he leaves
The healing benediction. With this strange virtue
He hath a heavenly gift of prophecy,
And sundry blessings hang about his throne   175
That speak him full of grace.

186–187 where nothing . . . where no one, except someone who may know nothing about what goes on, is ever
seen to smile.

189 not mark'd go unnoticed.

190 modern ecstasy commonplace expression of excitement.

193 Dying or ere they sicken dying unnaturally, not through
illness.

195 nice accurate.

197–198 That of an hour's age . . . The report of an hour-old
grief earns hisses for the speaker for telling stale news,
since new griefs occur every minute.

Enter Ross.

Macduff

                                    See, who comes here?

Malcolm

  My countryman; but yet I know him not.

Macduff

  My ever gentle cousin, welcome hither.

Malcolm

  I know him now: good God, betimes remove   180
  The means that makes us strangers!

Ross

                                        Sir, amen.

Macduff

  Stands Scotland where it did?

Ross

                              Alas, poor country!
  Almost afraid to know itself! It cannot   185
  Be call'd our mother, but our grave: where nothing,
  But who knows nothing, is once seen to smile;
  Where sighs and groans and shrieks that rend the air,
  Are made, not mark'd; where violent sorrow seems
  A modern ecstasy: the dead man's knell   190
  Is there scarce ask'd for who; and good men's lives
  Expire before the flowers in their caps,
  Dying or ere they sicken.

Macduff

                          O, relation
  Too nice, and yet too true!   195

Malcolm

                          What's the newest grief?

Ross

  That of an hour's age doth hiss the speaker;
  Each minute teems a new one.

Macduff

                              How does my wife?

208 **out** armed and in the field.
209 **witness'd the rather** all the more confirmed.

222 **latch** catch.

224 **fee-grief** a personal grief.

Ross
  Why, well.   200
Macduff
              And all my children?
Ross
                                        Well too.
Macduff
  The tyrant has not batter'd at their peace?
Ross
  No; they were well at peace when I did leave 'em.
Macduff
  Be not a niggard of your speech: how goes 't?   205
Ross
  When I came hither to transport the tidings,
  Which I have heavily borne, there ran a rumor
  Of many worthy fellows that were out;
  Which was to my belief witness'd the rather,
  For that I saw the tyrant's power a-foot: 210
  Now is the time of help; your eye in Scotland
  Would create soldiers, make our women fight,
  To doff their dire distresses.
Malcolm
                      Be 't their comfort
  We are coming thither: gracious England hath   215
  Lent us good Siward and ten thousand men;
  An older and a better soldier none
  That Christendom gives out.
Ross
                      Would I could answer
  This comfort with the like! But I have words   220
  That would be howl'd out in the desert air,
  Where hearing should not latch them.
Macduff
                      What concern they?
  The general cause? or is it a fee-grief
  Due to some single breast?   225

237 **the quarry of these murder'd deer** figurative, meaning the heap of murdered innocent bodies.

242 **o'erfraught** overburdened.

Ross

　　　　　　　　　No mind that's honest
But in it shares some woe, though the main part
Pertains to you alone.

Macduff

　　　　　　　　If it be mine,
Keep it not from me, quickly let me have it.　　　230

Ross

Let not your ears despise my tongue for ever,
Which shall possess them with the heaviest sound
That ever yet they heard.

Macduff

　　　　　　　　　Hum! I guess at it.

Ross

Your castle is surpris'd; your wife and babes　　　235
Savagely slaughter'd: to relate the manner,
Were, on the quarry of these murder'd deer,
To add the death of you.

Malcolm

　　　　　　　　Merciful heaven!
What, man! ne'er pull your hat upon your brows;　　　240
Give sorrow words: the grief that does not speak
Whispers the o'erfraught heart, and bids it break.

Macduff

My children too?

Ross

　　　　　　　Wife, children, servants, all
That could be found.　　　245

Macduff

　　　　　　　　And I must be from thence!
My wife kill'd too?

Ross

　　　　　　　I have said.

Malcolm

　　　　　　　　　Be comforted:

253 **hell-kite** The kite is a bird of prey.

275 **Our lack . . .** All we lack is the king's permission to leave.

277 **Put on their instruments** arm themselves. Malcolm's forces will have heavenly assistance, the war being a just one.

    Let's make us med'cines of our great revenge,   250
    To cure this deadly grief.

Macduff

    He has no children. All my pretty ones?
    Did you say all? O hell-kite! All?
    What, all my pretty chickens and their dam
    At one fell swoop?   255

Malcolm

    Dispute it like a man.

Macduff

                        I shall do so;
    But I must also feel it as a man:
    I cannot but remember such things were,
    That were most precious to me. Did heaven look on,   260
    And would not take their part? Sinful Macduff,
    They were all struck for thee! naught that I am,
    Not for their own demerits, but for mine,
    Fell slaughter on their souls: heaven rest them now!

Malcolm

    Be this the whetstone of your sword: let grief   265
    Convert to anger; blunt not the heart, enrage it.

Macduff

    O, I could play the woman with mine eyes,
    And braggart with my tongue! But, gentle heavens,
    Cut short all intermission; front to front
    Bring thou this fiend of Scotland and myself;   270
    Within my sword's length set him; if he 'scape,
    Heaven forgive him too!

Malcolm

                        This tune goes manly.
    Come, go we to the king; our power is ready;
    Our lack is nothing but our leave. Macbeth   275
    Is ripe for shaking, and the pow'rs above
    Put on their instruments. Receive what cheer you may;
    The night is long that never finds the day.

                                            [*Exeunt.*

9   **do the effects of watching**   act as though awake.

ACT V

*Enter a Doctor of Physic and a Waiting-
Gentlewoman.*

Doctor
I have two nights watched with you, but can perceive
no truth in your report. When was it she last walked?

Gentlewoman
Since his majesty went into the field, I have seen her
rise from her bed, throw her nightgown upon her,
unlock her closet, take forth paper, fold it, write   5
upon 't, read it, afterwards seal it, and again return
to bed; yet all this while in a most fast sleep.

Doctor
A great perturbation in nature, to receive at once the
benefit of sleep and do the effects of watching! In
this slumbery agitation, besides her walking and other   10
actual performances, what, at any time, have you
heard her say?

Gentlewoman
That, sir, which I will not report after her.

Doctor
You may to me, and 'tis most meet you should.

Gentlewoman
Neither to you nor any one, having no witness to   15
confirm my speech.

Enter Lady Macbeth, with a taper.

23   their sense is shut   Her eyes really perceive nothing.

Lo you, here she comes! This is her very guise, and,
upon my life, fast asleep. Observe her; stand close.

Doctor

How came she by that light?

Gentlewoman

Why, it stood by her: she has light by her contin-   20
ually; 'tis her command.

Doctor

You see, her eyes are open.

Gentlewoman

Aye, but their sense is shut.

Doctor

What is it she does now? Look, how she rubs her
hands.   25

Gentlewoman

It is an accustomed action with her, to seem thus
washing her hands: I have known her continue in this
a quarter of an hour.

Lady Macbeth

Yet here's a spot.

Doctor

Hark! she speaks: I will set down what comes from   30
her, to satisfy my remembrance the more strongly.

Lady Macbeth

Out, damned spot! out, I say! One: two: why, then
'tis time to do 't. Hell is murky. Fie, my lord, fie! a
soldier, and afeard? What need we fear who knows
it, when none can call our power to account? Yet who   35
would have thought the old man to have had so
much blood in him?

Doctor

Do you mark that?

Lady Macbeth

The thane of Fife had a wife; where is she now?
What, will these hands ne'er be clean? No more o'   40

43 **go to** go away.

that, my lord, no more o' that: you mar all with this
starting.

Doctor

Go to, go to; you have known what you should not.

Gentlewoman

She has spoke what she should not, I am sure of
that: heaven knows what she has known.   45

Lady Macbeth

Here's the smell of the blood still: all the perfumes of
Arabia will not sweeten this little hand. Oh, oh, oh!

Doctor

What a sigh is there! The heart is sorely charged.

Gentlewoman

I would not have such a heart in my bosom for the
dignity of the whole body.   50

Doctor

Well, well, well—

Gentlewoman

Pray God it be, sir.

Doctor

This disease is beyond my practice: yet I have known
those which have walked in their sleep who have died
holily in their beds.   55

Lady Macbeth

Wash your hands; put on your nightgown; look not
so pale: I tell you yet again, Banquo's buried; he cannot come out on 's grave.

Doctor

Even so?

Lady Macbeth

To bed, to bed; there's knocking at the gate: come,   60
come, come, come, give me your hand: what's done
cannot be undone: to bed, to bed, to bed.

[*Exit.*

68 **the divine** a minister.

72 **mated** bewildered.

3 **dear** heartfelt.
4–5 **Would to the bleeding . . .** would excite even a paralyzed man to bloody fierce battle.

Doctor

　　Will she go now to bed?

Gentlewoman

　　Directly.

Doctor

　　Foul whisperings are abroad: unnatural deeds   65
　　Do breed unnatural troubles: infected minds
　　To their deaf pillows will discharge their secrets:
　　More needs she the divine than the physician.
　　God, God forgive us all! Look after her;
　　Remove from her the means of all annoyance,   70
　　And still keep eyes upon her. So good night:
　　My mind she has mated and amazed my sight:
　　I think, but dare not speak.

Gentlewoman

　　　　　　　　　　　Good night, good doctor.
　　　　　　　　　　　　　　[*Exeunt.*

Scene 2. *The country near Dunsinane*

*Drum and colors. Enter Menteith, Caithness,
Angus, Lennox, and Soldiers.*

Menteith

　　The English power is near, led on by Malcolm,
　　His uncle Siward and the good Macduff:
　　Revenges burn in them; for their dear causes
　　Would to the bleeding and the grim alarm
　　Excite the mortified man.   5

Angus

　　　　　　　　　Near Birnam wood
　　Shall we well meet them; that way are they coming.

Caithness

　　Who knows if Donalbain be with his brother?

11 **unrough** unbearded.

17–18 **He cannot buckle his distemper'd cause / Within the belt of rule** Macbeth has lost control.

21 **minutely** every minute.
upbraid his faith-breach remind him of his own breach of faith.

27 **pester'd** tormented.

32 **the medicine of the sickly weal** a reference to Malcolm, who constitutes the cure for the ailing state.

36 **To dew** to water.

Lennox

   For certain, sir, he is not: I have a file
   Of all the gentry: there is Siward's son,   10
   And many unrough youths, that even now
   Protest their first of manhood.

Menteith

                       What does the tyrant?

Caithness

   Great Dunsinane he strongly fortifies:
   Some say he's mad; others, that lesser hate him,   15
   Do call it valiant fury: but, for certain,
   He cannot buckle his distemper'd cause
   Within the belt of rule.

Angus

               Now does he feel
   His secret murders sticking on his hands;   20
   Now minutely revolts upbraid his faith-breach;
   Those he commands move only in command,
   Nothing in love: now does he feel his title
   Hang loose about him, like a giant's robe
   Upon a dwarfish thief.   25

Menteith

               Who then shall blame
   His pester'd senses to recoil and start,
   When all that is within him does condemn
   Itself for being there?

Caithness

               Well, march we on,   30
   To give obedience where 'tis truly ow'd:
   Meet we the medicine of the sickly weal,
   And with him pour we, in our country's purge,
   Each drop of us.

Lennox

             Or so much as it needs   35
   To dew the sovereign flower and drown the weeds.
   Make we our march towards Birnam.

                    [*Exeunt, marching.*

8 English epicures a term of scorn. The English were sup-
posed to live lavishly.

11 loon fool.

17 patch stupid person.

Scene 3. Dunsinane. A room in the castle

Enter Macbeth, Doctor, and Attendants.

Macbeth
  Bring me no more reports; let them fly all:
  Till Birnam wood remove to Dunsinane
  I cannot taint with fear. What's the boy Malcolm?
  Was he not born of woman? The spirits that know
  All mortal consequences have pronounc'd me thus: 5
  "Fear not, Macbeth; no man that's born of woman
  Shall e'er have power upon thee." Then fly, false thanes,
  And mingle with the English epicures:
  The mind I sway by and the heart I bear
  Shall never sag with doubt nor shake with fear.   10

    Enter a Servant.

  The devil damn thee black, thou cream-fac'd loon!
  Where got'st thou that goose look?
Servant
  There is ten thousand—
Macbeth
               Geese, villain?
Servant
                      Soldiers, sir.   15
Macbeth
  Go prick thy face and over-red thy fear,
  Thou lily-liver'd boy. What soldiers, patch!
  Death of my soul! those linen cheeks of thine
  Are counselors to fear. What soldiers, whey-face!
Servant
  The English force, so please you.   20

23 push effort.
24 disseat dethrone.

26 sear withered.

40 moe more.
skirr scour.

Macbeth

　Take thy face hence.

　　　　　　　　　　　　　[Exit Servant.
　　　　　　Seyton!—I am sick at heart,
When I behold—Seyton, I say!—This push
Will cheer me ever, or disseat me now.
I have liv'd long enough: my way of life　　　　　25
Is fall'n into the sear, the yellow leaf,
And that which should accompany old age,
As honor, love, obedience, troops of friends,
I must not look to have; but, in their stead,
Curses, not loud but deep, mouth-honor, breath,　　30
Which the poor heart would fain deny, and dare not.
Seyton!

　　Enter Seyton.

Seyton

　What's your gracious pleasure?

Macbeth

　　　　　　　　　　What news more?

Seyton

　All is confirm'd, my lord, which was reported.　　35

Macbeth

　I'll fight, till from my bones my flesh be hack'd.
Give me my armor.

Seyton

　　　　　　'Tis not needed yet.

Macbeth

　I'll put it on.
Send out moe horses, skirr the country round;　　40
Hang those that talk of fear. Give me mine armor.
How does your patient, doctor?

Doctor

　　　　　　　　Not so sick, my lord,
As she is troubled with thick-coming fancies,
That keep her from her rest.　　　　　　　45

49 **Raze out** erase.
50 **oblivious** causing oblivion.

55 **physic** medicine.

58–60 **cast** / **The water of my land** . . . diagnose the disease my country suffers from and cure it.

68 **bane** destruction.

Macbeth

                              Cure her of that.
Canst thou not minister to a mind diseas'd,
Pluck from the memory a rooted sorrow,
Raze out the written troubles of the brain,
And with some sweet oblivious antidote   50
Cleanse the stuff'd bosom of that perilous stuff
Which weighs upon the heart?

Doctor

                              Therein the patient
Must minister to himself.

Macbeth

Throw physic to the dogs, I'll none of it.   55
Come, put mine armor on; give me my staff.
Seyton, send out. Doctor, the thanes fly from me.
Come, sir, dispatch. If thou couldst, doctor, cast
The water of my land, find her disease,
And purge it to a sound and pristine health,   60
I would applaud thee to the very echo,
That should applaud again. Pull 't off, I say.
What rhubarb, senna, or what purgative drug,
Would scour these English hence? Hear'st thou of
      them?

Doctor

Aye, my good lord; your royal preparation   65
Makes us hear something.

Macbeth

                         Bring it after me.
I will not be afraid of death and bane
Till Birnam forest come to Dunsinane.

Doctor

[*Aside*]   Were I from Dunsinane away and clear,   70
Profit again should hardly draw me here.
                                          [*Exeunt.*

15 **advantage** opportunity.
16 **more and less** those of higher and lower station.

19 **censures** opinions.
20 **true event** actual outcome.

Scene 4. *Country near Birnam wood*

Drum and colors. Enter Malcolm, old Siward and his Son, Macduff, Menteith, Caithness, Angus, Lennox, Ross and Soldiers, marching.

Malcolm
  Cousins, I hope the days are near at hand
  That chambers will be safe.

Menteith
                                        We doubt it nothing.

Siward
  What wood is this before us?

Menteith
                                        The wood of Birnam.   5

Malcolm
  Let every soldier hew him down a bough,
  And bear 't before him: thereby shall we shadow
  The numbers of our host, and make discovery
  Err in report of us.

Soldiers
                              It shall be done.   10

Siward
  We learn no other but the confident tyrant
  Keeps still in Dunsinane, and will endure
  Our setting down before 't.

Malcolm
                                    'Tis his main hope:
  For where there is advantage to be given,   15
  Both more and less have given him the revolt,
  And none serve with him but constrained things
  Whose hearts are absent too.

Macduff
                                    Let our just censures
  Attend the true event, and put we on   20
  Industrious soldiership.

24 **What we shall say ...**   what we shall claim as ours and
   what we will actually possess.
26 **certain issue strokes ...**   Only actual blows that are struck
   in battle will bring a definite outcome.
27 **which**   a pronoun referring to *strokes* in line 26.

4 **ague**   pestilence.
5 **forc'd**   reinforced.

12 **my fell of hair**   the hair on my skin.
13 **treatise**   story.

Siward

                    The time approaches,
        That will with due decision make us know
        What we shall say we have and what we owe.
        Thoughts speculative their unsure hopes relate,   25
        But certain issue strokes must arbitrate:
        Towards which advance the war.
                              [*Exeunt, marching.*

Scene 5. Dunsinane. Within the castle

*Enter Macbeth, Seyton, and Soldiers, with drum
and colors.*

Macbeth

        Hang out our banners on the outward walls;
        The cry is still "They come;" our castle's strength
        Will laugh a siege to scorn: here let them lie
        Till famine and the ague eat them up:
        Were they not forc'd with those that should be ours,   5
        We might have met them dareful, beard to beard,
        And beat them backward home.
                              [A *cry of women within.*
                              What is that noise?

Seyton

        It is the cry of women, my good lord.
                                                [*Exit.*

Macbeth

        I have almost forgot the taste of fears: 10
        The time has been, my senses would have cool'd
        To hear a night-shriek, and my fell of hair
        Would at a dismal treatise rouse and stir
        As life were in 't: I have supp'd full with horrors;

16 start startle.

Direness, familiar to my slaughterous thoughts,   15
Cannot once start me.

  Reenter Seyton.

                              Wherefore was that cry?

Seyton
The queen, my lord, is dead.

Macbeth
She should have died hereafter;
There would have been a time for such a word.   20
Tomorrow, and tomorrow, and tomorrow,
Creeps in this petty pace from day to day,
To the last syllable of recorded time;
And all our yesterdays have lighted fools
The way to dusty death. Out, out, brief candle!   25
Life's but a walking shadow, a poor player
That struts and frets his hour upon the stage
And then is heard no more: it is a tale
Told by an idiot, full of sound and fury,
Signifying nothing.   30

  Enter a Messenger.

Thou com'st to use thy tongue; thy story quickly.

Messenger
Gracious my lord,
I should report that which I say I saw,
But know not how to do it.

Macbeth
                              Well, say, sir.   35

Messenger
As I did stand my watch upon the hill,
I look'd toward Birnam, and anon, methought,
The wood began to move.

Macbeth
                              Liar and slave!

45 **cling** wither, waste away.
   sooth truth.
47 **pull in resolution** check or hold back my determination.
48 **doubt** fear.
   equivocation a statement of ambiguous or double meaning.

56 **wrack** ruin.
57 **harness** armor.

Messenger

   Let me endure your wrath, if 't be not so: 40
   Within this three mile may you see it coming;
   I say, a moving grove.

Macbeth

                 If thou speak'st false,
   Upon the next tree shalt thou hang alive,
   Till famine cling thee: if thy speech be sooth,   45
   I care not if thou dost for me as much.
   I pull in resolution, and begin
   To doubt th' equivocation of the fiend
   That lies like truth: "Fear not, till Birnam wood
   Do come to Dunsinane"; and now a wood   50
   Comes toward Dunsinane. Arm, arm, and out!
   If this which he avouches does appear,
   There is nor flying hence nor tarrying here.
   I 'gin to be a-weary of the sun,
   And wish th' estate o' the world were now undone.   55
   Ring the alarum-bell! Blow, wind! come, wrack!
   At least we'll die with harness on our back.

                                [Exeunt.

Scene 6. Dunsinane. Before the castle

*Drum and colors. Enter Malcolm, old Siward,
Macduff, and their Army, with boughs.*

Malcolm

   Now near enough; your leavy screens throw down,
   And show like those you are. You, worthy uncle,
   Shall, with my cousin, your right noble son,
   Lead our first battle: worthy Macduff and we
   Shall take upon 's what else remains to do,   5
   According to our order.

11 **harbingers** forerunners.

2 **bear-like** a reference to the sport of bear-baiting, in which dogs attacked a bear tied to a stake.

Siward
                  Fare you well.
  Do we but find the tyrant's power tonight,
  Let us be beaten, if we cannot fight.
Macduff
  Make all our trumpets speak; give them all breath,   10
  Those clamorous harbingers of blood and death.
                        [*Exeunt.*

Scene 7. Another part of the field

  Alarums. Enter Macbeth.

Macbeth
  They have tied me to a stake; I cannot fly,
  But bear-like I must fight the course. What's he
  That was not born of woman? Such a one
  Am I to fear, or none.

    Enter young Siward.

Young Siward
  What is thy name?   5
Macbeth
                  Thou 'lt be afraid to hear it.
Young Siward
  No; though thou call'st thyself a hotter name
  Than any is in hell.
Macbeth
                My name's Macbeth.
Young Siward
  The devil himself could not pronounce a title   10
  More hateful to mine ear.
Macbeth
               No, nor more fearful.

22 **staves** spears.

26 **bruited** proclaimed.

28 **render'd** surrendered.

31 **itself professes** declares itself.

34 **strike beside us** strike without really trying to hit us.

Young Siward

　Thou liest, abhorred tyrant; with my sword
　I'll prove the lie thou speak'st.
　　　　　　[They fight, and young Siward is slain.

Macbeth

　　　　　　　　Thou wast born of woman.　15
　But swords I smile at, weapons laugh to scorn,
　Brandish'd by man that's of a woman born.
　　　　　　　　　　　[Exit.

　　Alarums. Enter Macduff.

Macduff

　That way the noise is. Tyrant, show thy face!
　If thou be'st slain and with no stroke of mine,
　My wife and children's ghosts will haunt me still.　20
　I cannot strike at wretched kerns, whose arms
　Are hir'd to bear their staves: either thou, Macbeth,
　Or else my sword, with an unbatter'd edge,
　I sheathe again undeeded. There thou shouldst be;
　By this great clatter, one of greatest note　25
　Seems bruited: let me find him, fortune!
　And more I beg not.
　　　　　　　　　[Exit. Alarums.

　　Enter Malcolm and old Siward.

Siward

　This way, my lord; the castle's gently render'd:
　The tyrant's people on both sides do fight;
　The noble thanes do bravely in the war;　30
　The day almost itself professes yours,
　And little is to do.

Malcolm

　　　　　　We have met with foes
　That strike beside us.

Siward

　　　　　　Enter, sir, the castle.　35
　　　　　　　　　[Exeunt. Alarum.

1 **the Roman fool** a reference to the Roman custom of committing suicide rather than suffering defeat.

12 **intrenchant** invulnerable.

20 **Untimely ripp'd** delivered as in a Caesarian operation, not naturally born.

Scene 8. *Another part of the field*

Enter Macbeth.

Macbeth
> Why should I play the Roman fool, and die
> On mine own sword? whiles I see lives, the gashes
> Do better upon them.

> *Enter Macduff.*

Macduff
>   Turn, hell-hound, turn!

Macbeth
> Of all men else I have avoided thee: 5
> But get thee back; my soul is too much charg'd
> With blood of thine already.

Macduff
>   I have no words:
> My voice is in my sword, thou bloodier villain
> Than terms can give thee out!   10
>   [*They fight.*

Macbeth
>   Thou losest labor:
> As easy mayst thou the intrenchant air
> With thy keen sword impress as make me bleed:
> Let fall thy blade on vulnerable crests;
> I bear a charmed life, which must not yield   15
> To one of woman born.

Macduff
>   Despair thy charm,
> And let the angel whom thou still hast serv'd
> Tell thee, Macduff was from his mother's womb
> Untimely ripp'd.   20

Macbeth
> Accursed be that tongue that tells me so,

24 **palter** deceive.

30 **Painted upon a pole** his picture painted and set up on a pole for popular display.

34 **baited** assailed.

For it hath cow'd my better part of man!
And be these juggling fiends no more believ'd,
That palter with us in a double sense,
That keep the word of promise to our ear,　　　　25
And break it to our hope. I'll not fight with thee.

Macduff

Then yield thee, coward,
And live to be the show and gaze o' the time:
We'll have thee, as our rarer monsters are,
Painted upon a pole, and underwrit,　　　　30
"Here may you see the tyrant."

Macbeth

　　　　　　　　　　I will not yield,
To kiss the ground before young Malcolm's feet,
And to be baited with the rabble's curse.
Though Birnam wood be come to Dunsinane,　　　　35
And thou oppos'd, being of no woman born,
Yet I will try the last: before my body
I throw my warlike shield: lay on, Macduff;
And damn'd be him that first cries "Hold, enough!"
　　　　　　　　　[Exeunt, fighting. Alarums

*Retreat. Flourish. Enter, with drum and colors,
Malcolm, old Siward, Ross, the other Thanes, and
Soldiers.*

Malcolm

I would the friends we miss were safe arriv'd.　　　　40

Siward

Some must go off: and yet, by these I see,
So great a day as this is cheaply bought.

Malcolm

Macduff is missing, and your noble son.

Ross

Your son, my lord, has paid a soldier's debt:

62 **parted** departed.
    score account.

65 **the time is free** We are freed from tyranny.
66 **compass'd** surrounded.
    thy kingdom's pearl the kingdom's riches (the royal
    thanes).

He only liv'd but till he was a man;　　　45
The which no sooner had his prowess confirm'd
In the unshrinking station where he fought,
But like a man he died.

Siward

Then he is dead?

Ross

Aye, and brought off the field: your cause of sorrow　　50
Must not be measur'd by his worth, for then
It hath no end.

Siward

Had he his hurts before?

Ross

Aye, on the front.

Siward

Why then, God's soldier be he!　　55
Had I as many sons as I have hairs,
I would not wish them to a fairer death:
And so his knell is knoll'd.

Malcolm

He's worth more sorrow,
And that I'll spend for him.　　60

Siward

He's worth no more:
They say he parted well and paid his score:
And so God be with him! Here comes newer comfort.

Reenter Macduff, with Macbeth's head.

Macduff

Hail, king! for so thou art: behold, where stands
Th' usurper's cursed head: the time is free:　　65
I see thee compass'd with thy kingdom's pearl,
That speak my salutation in their minds;
Whose voices I desire aloud with mine:
Hail, King of Scotland!

72–73 reckon with . . . count up the services you have rendered and repay you for them.

75–76 What's more to do ... whatever else remains, which will soon be done.

79 Producing forth bringing from out of hiding.

83 Grace divine Grace.

All

Hail, King of Scotland! 70

[*Flourish.*

Malcolm

We shall not spend a large expense of time
Before we reckon with your several loves,
And make us even with you. My thanes and kinsmen,
Henceforth be earls, the first that ever Scotland
In such an honor nam'd. What's more to do, 75
Which would be planted newly with the time,
As calling home our exil'd friends abroad
That fled the snares of watchful tyranny,
Producing forth the cruel ministers
Of this dead butcher and his fiend-like queen, 80
Who, as 'tis thought, by self and violent hands
Took off her life; this, and what needful else
That calls upon us, by the grace of Grace
We will perform in measure, time and place:
So thanks to all at once and to each one, 85
Whom we invite to see us crown'd at Scone.

[*Flourish. Exeunt.*

READER'S GUIDE

Solomon Schlakman

INTRODUCTION

Many of the English and American classics which your parents read and studied in high school are no longer in the curriculum. They have been replaced by more modern or contemporary works which have more relevance to our own time and hence have proved more interesting to young people. Nevertheless, there has been little if any tendency to eliminate from the schools the reading of those major tragedies of Shakespeare which have been read for centuries — particularly *Macbeth* and *Hamlet*. These works have apparently retained their excitement and appeal for students. Shakespeare's genius appears to be as relevant and arresting today as it has always been in the past.

Once you begin reading *Macbeth* you will quickly see why this is so. It is probably the most powerful murder story ever devised. But its appeal is more universal and profound than the surface story might indicate. Like all of Shakespeare's great works, it plumbs human character and the human condition, and through the power of its language, the play inevitably involves every reader in the anguish of human suffering which it depicts. Everything in the play — the setting, the action, the characters, the lines they speak and the images and pictures which their language evokes, the very pace and rhythm of the speeches and the plot — all combine to form an overpowering vision of a world of evil in which not only the players but also the readers and audience are inescapably caught up.

The material in the *Reader's Guide* which follows is designed to make you more consciously aware than you might otherwise be of the elements and forces in the play which work to make it such a memorable psychological and esthetic experience.

Shakespeare wrote poetic drama. His genius lay not only in his understanding of human nature and human problems; equally important was his unsurpassed gift for language, which heightened, intensified, and vivified whatever action or feelings or ideas he depicted in his plays.

Two strands of questions comprise the *Reader's Guide*. The first strand directs attention to the elements in the action, speeches, and characterization which serve to create the vision of a nightmare world brought on by Macbeth's commitment to evil. The second strand of questions is concerned with specific elements of poetic and stage craftsmanship which work with the action to render this vision of evil so powerful and affecting.

Some preliminary explanation of certain literary techniques frequently referred to in the *Reader's Guide* may be helpful to you at this point.

Reference is frequently made to **imagery** or **figurative language**. These terms describe a writer's use of striking sense impressions or comparisons to heighten or render more vivid the thought or feeling that is being expressed. Most often this language takes the form of a directly stated comparison (a simile) or an implied comparison (a metaphor).

Early in the play, for example, Macbeth comments on the fact that the witches have suddenly vanished from sight. He uses a **simile** to express his feeling about how they have vanished (Act I, Scene 3, lines 82–83):

" . . . and what seem'd corporal [substantial] melted
As breath into the wind."

A well-known example of **metaphor** occurs in Macbeth's famous description of the meaninglessness of life, spoken near the end of the play (Act V, Scene 5, lines 28–30):

" . . . it [life] is a tale
Told by an idiot, full of sound and fury,
Signifying nothing."

Another literary device frequently alluded to in the *Reader's Guide* is the use of **antithesis** and **paradox**. More than the other plays of Shakespeare, *Macbeth* seems to abound in antithesis and paradox — for a good reason: these related devices involve the use of opposites and contradictions, and the dramatic vision that *Macbeth* offers is that of a world in which order, regularity, logic, and conventional and accepted values have all been overturned and destroyed.

Antithesis is a statement that joins opposing or contradictory ideas. An early example is found in Lady Macbeth's description of her husband's character (Act I, Scene 5, lines 21–22):

> ". . . wouldst not play false,
> And yet wouldst wrongly win. . . ."

Paradox is a special form of antithesis in which *apparently* contradictory ideas are expressed closely together. The ideas are only apparently contradictory, because on examination in a certain context, they contain an element of truth. A striking example of paradox occurs in the first scene, when the witches set the tone for the rest of the play (Act I, Scene 1, line 11):

> "Fair is foul, and foul is fair."

These ideas seem contradictory; however, in the world of the witches (and in the world of the play as it will develop), there is truth in them, because normal moral values are inverted, or turned around.

Another literary device frequently referred to in the *Reader's Guide* is irony. An ironical statement implies the opposite of what it seems to say. In all irony there is a surface element of oppositeness or inconsistency with what the reader or listener knows to be true. The underlying truth is rendered more emphatic because of the ironical manner in which it has been expressed. For example, you may say to someone who has rejected your plea for assistance, "You certainly are helpful, aren't you?" You mean, of course, the opposite of what you have said, your meaning probably having been expressed through your tone of voice.

Most frequently in *Macbeth* the reader will find an especially effective form of irony called dramatic irony. This occurs in a situation when the reader or audience is aware of more meaning or significance in a statement than the character who makes the statement is aware of. Usually, the reader, having information which the character lacks, knows the real truth to be the opposite of what the character assumes.

An early example of dramatic irony in *Macbeth* occurs in Act I, Scene 4. The king, Duncan, has ordered the execution of a traitor, Cawdor. Speaking of his error in trusting Cawdor, Duncan says (lines 15—16):

> "He was a gentleman on whom I built
> An absolute trust."

He turns then to Macbeth and speaks to him in terms of the greatest praise, calling him "worthiest cousin." (line 17) The reader knows what Duncan does not know — that Macbeth himself has entertained thoughts of killing Duncan to become king.

The story of Macbeth is based on Shakespeare's reading of a historical book popular in his time called *Chronicles of England, Scotland, and Ireland*, written by Raphael Holinshed. The action takes place in Scotland in the middle of the eleventh century, at a time when Scotland was still an independent country. Shakespeare made changes freely in the events of the story and in his characterizations to suit his own dramatic purposes.

QUESTIONS

Act I, Scenes 1 to 4

THE NIGHTMARE WORLD OF MACBETH

1. The first scene of the play is very brief, but rich in its hints about the kind of world we shall encounter as the play unfolds.

    a. What effect would the initial setting and the lighting (as suggested by the stage directions) have on the viewing audience?

    b. What feelings and what anticipation would be stirred in the audience by the characters in the scene and the words they speak? Note especially the last two lines spoken in chorus.

2. What impressions of Macbeth's character are created, before his actual appearance in the play, by the details of the battle accounts of the sergeant and Ross in Scene 2?

3. How are our first impressions of the witches and their role in the play affected by the story in Scene 3 of the sailor's wife and her husband?

4. The first words Macbeth utters in the play echo a line already spoken. (Act I, Scene 3, line 38) What significant effect does Shakespeare create through this device?

5. What prophecies do the witches make to Macbeth? What prophecies do they offer to Banquo? Which one of the prophecies that comes as a shock to Macbeth does the reader already know has been fulfilled?

6. Observing Macbeth's immediate reactions to the prophecies, Banquo says, "Good sir, why do you start and seem to fear / Things that do sound so fair?" What reasons can you think of to explain why Macbeth is startled and apparently fearful when he hears the prophecies?

7. Note, in Scene 3, how both Macbeth and Banquo address the witches and how they react to what they hear. Do they seem alike or different in their manner of speaking and in their reactions? Specify the similarities or differences you observe.

8. What do Banquo's remarks about "the instruments of darkness" tell us about his character at this point? (Scene 3, lines 129—133) Explain the relevance of these remarks to the thoughts which Macbeth later utters in his soliloquies.

9. What do we learn about Macbeth's secret thoughts from his brief aside, "Two truths are told..."? (Scene 3, lines 135—137)

10. The most significant inkling about Macbeth's secret thoughts comes in the soliloquy beginning, "This supernatural soliciting...." (Scene 3, lines 138—150)

   a. What is the suggestion "whose horrid image doth unfix my hair"?

   b. What moral conflict appears to exist in Macbeth's mind? Quote and explain the lines in which this conflict is expressed.

   c. What conclusions about Macbeth's character can you draw from this soliloquy? Consider especially this question: Why does the thought of killing Duncan affect in this way the man who has killed so many others on the battlefield, notably Macdonwald?

11. The reader's reaction to Macbeth's conflict of mind depends to a great degree on the impressions he has derived of Duncan's qualities as a person and a king. What impressions of Duncan do you get from his utterances and behavior in the following instances?

   a. His treatment of the wounded sergeant. (Scene 2, lines 47—48)

   b. His announcement of Macbeth's reward. (Scene 2, lines 72—76)

   c. His remarks about Cawdor. (Scene 4, lines 13—16)

   d. His greeting of Macbeth after the latter's victory. (Scene 4, lines 17—24 and 31—33)

e. His comments to Banquo about Macbeth. (Scene 4, lines 61—65)

12. Review Macbeth's thinking about his future course of action as it is revealed in the two speeches noted below, and answer the questions that follow:

(1) "If chance will have me king, why, chance may crown me, Without my stir." (Scene 3, lines 152—153)

(2) The speech beginning "The Prince of Cumberland! that is a step. . . ." (Scene 4, lines 55—60)

a. Has Macbeth's mind remained steadfast, or has it changed? What significant event affected Macbeth's decision in the second speech?

b. How does Macbeth seem to *feel* about the decision he expresses in the second soliloquy above? What words indicate that feeling?

c. What inferences about Macbeth's character do you draw from his shifting thoughts on the question of murder?

SHAKESPEARE'S LANGUAGE AND CRAFT

13. In what ways do the actual words of the witches in the first scene help to create the feeling of a nightmare world of evil and confusion? What particularly is the effect of the antithesis and paradox in the last lines?

14. The language of *Macbeth* abounds in further instances of antithesis and paradox. This multiplying of contradictions in the language of the play serves to strengthen the feeling of a world without clear order, a world of confusion and uncertainties. Point out three additional examples of such contradictions in the witches' prophecies to Banquo, and explain their effect on the audience or reader.

15. What example of antithesis do you find in Banquo's warning to Macbeth about "The instruments of darkness"? (Scene 3, lines 129—133)

16. In the soliloquy in which Macbeth explicitly ponders for the first time the possibility of murder, explain the force and meaning of the images in the following lines:

a.   ". . .why do I yield to that suggestion
            Whose horrid image doth unfix my hair
            And make my seated heart knock at my ribs,
            Against the use of nature?"

                                    (Scene 3, lines 142—145)

b.   "My thought, whose murder yet is but fantastical,
            Shakes so my single state of man that function
            Is smother'd in surmise, and nothing is
            But what is not."   (Scene 3, lines 147—150)

17. As the play proceeds, the reader will find repeated imagery based on "clothing," the significance of which imagery gradually emerges more clearly.

a. Explain the "clothing" metaphor in the following statement of Macbeth:

            "The thane of Cawdor lives: why do you dress me
            In borrow'd robes?"   (Scene 3, lines 112—113)

b. Explain the "clothing" metaphor in this statement of Banquo, taking into account the context in which it is spoken:

            "New honors come upon him,
            Like our strange garments, cleave not to their mold
            But with the aid of use." (Scene 3, lines 154—156)

18. Knowing Macbeth's secret hopes and thoughts, the alert audience and reader will appreciate the dramatic irony in many of Duncan's utterances.

a. Note Duncan's statement about the traitor Cawdor:

            "There's no art
            To find the mind's construction in the face."

                                    (Scene 4, lines 13—14)

Then note the greeting to Macbeth which immediately follows. What dramatic irony does Shakespeare provide here?

b. What further instances of dramatic irony can you find in

Duncan's remarks about Macbeth in subsequent parts of Scene 4?

Act I, Scenes 5 to 7

THE NIGHTMARE WORLD OF MACBETH

1. What comparisons between Lady Macbeth's character and that of Macbeth are suggested by each of the following?

a. Her first statement after reading Macbeth's letter. (Scene 5, lines 15—16)

b. The intention she announces in lines 25—30 of the same soliloquy.

2. A key soliloquy in our understanding of Lady Macbeth is that which begins, "The raven himself is hoarse . . . ." (Scene 5, line 42)

a. In what way do the specific images that dominate this soliloquy sustain the impression of a nightmare world?

b. Does the content of this soliloquy support the interpretation of Lady Macbeth as a thoroughly and unnaturally cruel, bloodthirsty woman? Do you find evidence for a different interpretation?

3. How do Lady Macbeth's greeting to her husband and her conversation with him (Scene 5, lines 59—82) demonstrate further the differences in their characters?

4. Lady Macbeth has told Macbeth to "look like the innocent flower, / But be the serpent under 't." How does she herself carry out this role in Scene 6 when Duncan arrives?

5. Macbeth's soliloquy at the start of Scene 7, in which he considers again the question of murder, provides an important further insight into his character, especially as it compares with Lady Macbeth's character.

a. What difference in his character is suggested by the fact that he engages in these thoughts?

b. What argument for or against the murder does Macbeth consider in the first part of the soliloquy, lines 1—12?

c. What argument does Macbeth advance in the next section of the soliloquy, lines 12—16?

d. What final argument is presented in his imaginative depiction of the general effect of the crime (lines 16—25)? In what way are his fundamental feelings revealed in these lines?

e. What do the last four lines of the soliloquy tell us about Macbeth's view of his own ambition to be king?

f. At this point in the play, what is Macbeth's decision on the question of murder? In what lines does he express that decision to Lady Macbeth?

6. Read carefully Lady Macbeth's responses to Macbeth's decision (lines 38—64) and recall the intention she expressed in Scene 5, lines 25—30. How do her words here carry out that intention?

7. The nature of the arguments Lady Macbeth uses to incite Macbeth to the act of murder shows her to be astutely aware of his character.

a. What aspect of his character does she appeal to in lines 38—42?

b. What aspect of his character does she appeal to in lines 42—49?

c. What aspect of his character does she appeal to in lines 52—64?

8. What plan has Lady Macbeth devised for the murder?

9. How would you at this point summarize the characters of Macbeth and Lady Macbeth?

SHAKESPEARE'S LANGUAGE AND CRAFT

10. The sense of inverted values, of moral confusion and disorder, is sustained in the play by further examples of antithesis in the language. What examples can you find in Lady Macbeth's first soliloquy at the opening of Scene 5? Explain the lines you cite.

11. What further significant example of antithesis can you find in Lady Macbeth's instructions to Macbeth? (Scene 5, lines 71–74)

12. The sense of a nightmare world is strongly reinforced in Lady Macbeth's key soliloquy beginning, "The raven himself is hoarse. . . ." (Scene 5, lines 42–58) How does the succession of images in this soliloquy convey that sense?

13. Scene 6 contains very little that is essential to the action of the play. Do you think that it might be omitted without loss, or do you believe it has some genuine dramatic value? Explain your answer. (Observe the note on *martlet*, page 34.)

14. Reread the opening lines of Macbeth's soliloquy beginning, "If it were done when 'tis done. . . ." (Scene 7, lines 1–28)

a. Explain the meaning of the opening sentence, with special attention to the meanings of the word *done*.

b. How does Macbeth's image of "trammeling" support the idea expressed in the opening lines?

c. Many astute readers have commented on the special artistry of the first four lines of this soliloquy. The pace of the words and their sound seem remarkably matched to the sense or meaning. Can you point out how this is so?

d. Macbeth uses particularly striking and effective imagery to convey his picture of the reaction of the general population to the murder of Duncan. (Scene 7, lines 16–25) Identify the key images and comment on their effectiveness.

15. Another metaphor of "clothing" is expressed by Macbeth in his dialogue with Lady Macbeth, as an argument against committing murder. What is the meaning of this metaphor, which begins "and I have bought / Golden opinions . . ."? (lines 34–37)

16. Which of the images used by Lady Macbeth in Scene 7 to overcome Macbeth's scruples was the most forceful and memorable to you? Explain its significance.

Act II

THE NIGHTMARE WORLD OF MACBETH

1. Up to this point Banquo, unlike Macbeth, has represented honesty, integrity, and order. What further light on Banquo is shed by each of these passages?

a. The four lines beginning "A heavy summons lies like lead upon me. . . ." (Scene 1, lines 7—10)

b. That part of the dialogue with Macbeth, Scene 1, lines 24—36. (What offer does Macbeth seem to make? Would Banquo's response be encouraging or discouraging to him?)

2. How do you explain the appearance of the dagger apparition, in terms of Macbeth's psychology as you know it? Comment on such specific details of that apparition as seem especially significant and revealing to you.

3. How would you describe Lady Macbeth's state of mind as she awaits the outcome of the murder attempt? What is revealing in her statement, "Had he not resembled / My father as he slept, I had done 't"? (Scene 2, lines 13—14)

4. Compare the attitudes of Macbeth and Lady Macbeth when he returns from the murder chamber and explains what happened. Consider these questions:

a. What is significant about Macbeth's preoccupation with the word "Amen"?

b. What is Macbeth implying about himself in his remarks about sleep? (Scene 2, lines 43—52)

c. What part of the murder plan did Macbeth fail to carry out? Why does he refuse to remedy the omission?

d. Reread Macbeth's lines beginning, "What hands are here?" (Scene 2, lines 71—75) What qualities of Macbeth already

212

noted do we observe in these lines? What is he saying about his future?

e. How would you describe the role Lady Macbeth plays in response to all of the above reactions and statements of Macbeth? In the light of all you know about her, what comment would you make on the fact that she must play such a role?

5. Observe the language in which Macduff expresses his feelings on the discovery of Duncan's murder. (Scene 3, lines 69—88) How does his language prophetically express the contrast between Scotland as it was under Duncan and as it will be as a result of Macbeth's evil act?

6. Consider the actions and words of each of the following characters as the murder is discovered and announced. (Scene 3) Do these reactions seem to promise success for Macbeth and Lady Macbeth, or do they portend difficulties?

    a. Macbeth himself.

    b. Lady Macbeth. (Why do you suppose she faints when she does?)

    c. Macduff. (What might be implied by his question to Macbeth, Scene 3, line 123, "Wherefore did you so?")

    d. Banquo.

    e. Malcolm and Donalbain.

7. In the light of the play's development, what purpose is served by the conversation between the Old Man and Ross at the beginning of Scene 4?

8. What is significant about Macduff's statement that he will not go to Scone?

SHAKESPEARE'S LANGUAGE AND CRAFT

9. In each of the following instances, how did Shakespeare arrange and manipulate details of setting to intensify the sense of nightmare horror?

a. The description of the night as Macbeth sees it in the latter part of his dagger soliloquy. (Scene 1, lines 57—69)

b. Lady Macbeth's reference to the noise she hears. (Scene 2, lines 3—4)

c. The remarks of Lennox about the night, uttered just before the murder is discovered. (Scene 3, lines 58—65)

10. At four points near the end of Scene 2, the audience is made aware of a loud knocking somewhere outside the court where Macbeth and Lady Macbeth are absorbed in their crime.

a. What is the dramatic effect of this knocking at this point in the play?

b. What is the dramatic effect of Macbeth's last words in this scene: "Wake Duncan with thy knocking! I would thou couldst!"?

11. Irony contributes to the mounting dramatic effect of the scenes in Act II. Explain what irony may be found in each of these passages:

a. Lady Macbeth's statement, "A little water clears us of this deed: / How easy is it, then!" (Scene 2, lines 80—81)

b. The humorous speeches of the porter in which he *pretends* to be a porter at the gates of Hell.

c. Macbeth's speech expressing to the other lords his pretended regret at the murder of Duncan. (Scene 3, lines 103—108)

12. In the light of earlier references to "clothing" imagery, what continuing significance do you see in Macduff's statement to Ross?

> "Well, may you see things well done there: adieu!
> Lest our old robes sit easier than our new!"
>
> (Scene 4, lines 48—49)

Act III, Scenes 1 to 3

THE NIGHTMARE WORLD OF MACBETH

1. Up to this point in the play, Banquo has been a man of the utmost integrity. In the light of his soliloquy at the opening of Act III, would you say there is evidence of change, or does he seem to continue in his original role? Support and explain your answer.

2. What intention with regard to Banquo seems to be implied in Macbeth's soliloquy? (Scene 1, lines 52—76) What are the specific reasons Macbeth offers for this intention?

3. How are these intentions confirmed in the conversation with the murderers in Scene 1? What specifically is the plan Macbeth has devised?

4. In Scenes 1 and 2 we discern significant changes in Macbeth's character and in his relationship with Lady Macbeth. What evidence of these changes do you see in each of the following instances?

    a. The decision Macbeth has come to about Banquo.

    b. Lady Macbeth's disturbed question to Macbeth, "Why do you keep alone, / Of sorriest fancies your companions making?"

    c. The manner in which Macbeth speaks to Lady Macbeth about Banquo. (Scene 2, lines 32—61)

5. Compare Lady Macbeth's secret thoughts when she is alone (Scene 2, lines 6—9) with her remarks that immediately follow when Macbeth enters (lines 10—14). What do these two passages reveal about Lady Macbeth's actual state of mind now that she is queen, and the role she feels she must play in her relationship to her husband? Note also in this connection her further statements in the same scene.

6. Earlier in the play, Macbeth made two significant prophecies of a nightmare future for himself:

(1) "Macbeth shall sleep no more." (Act II, Scene 2, line 52)

(2)   "... this my hand will rather
The multitudinous seas incarnadine,
Making the green one red."
(Act II, Scene 2, lines 73—75)

Find specific passages in Scenes 1 and 2 of Act III which show that these prophecies are being borne out even though his ambition seems to have been achieved. Relate each passage specifically to either of these prophecies.

7. In Scene 3 the plan of Macbeth is carried out by the murderers. In what respect is it successful? In what respect is it unsuccessful?

SHAKESPEARE'S LANGUAGE AND CRAFT

8. Macbeth's soliloquy, in which he contemplates why he wants Banquo out of the way, rises toward the close to a pitch of dramatic intensity which is created largely through the use of vivid metaphors. Identify some of the key metaphors in these lines (Scene 1, lines 65—76) and explain how they serve to heighten the expression of Macbeth's feelings.

9. The pervading sense of a dark and anguished world of horror is sustained in these scenes, particularly in Macbeth's speeches to Lady Macbeth, in which he describes his own state of mind and his sense of the world he inhabits. Find two or three such passages in Scene 2 of Act III and comment on the key images in each passage which strike you as particularly vivid and effective.

10. Scene 2 contains further examples of Shakespeare's use of antithesis to sustain the feeling of a confused world in which opposites and contradictions seem to prevail.

    a. What example of such antithesis do you find in Lady Macbeth's private thoughts expressed at the start of this scene?

b. Find and explain another example of antithesis in Macbeth's last remarks in the same scene.

11. One of the types of significant recurrent imagery in the play is that which deals with false surfaces or appearances. Earlier examples of such imagery were these:

> ". . . look like the innocent flower,
> But be the serpent under 't."
>
> (Act I, Scene 5, lines 73–74)

> "False face must hide what the false heart doth know."   (Act I, Scene 7, line 92)

Find and explain another example of such imagery in Macbeth's instructions to Lady Macbeth in Scene 2.

Act III, Scenes 4 to 6

THE NIGHTMARE WORLD OF MACBETH

1. The stage directions for this "banquet" scene are rather sparse. Keeping in mind that this banquet is probably Macbeth's first state celebration of his coming to power, what details of costume, stage setting, and lighting would you provide for if you were producing this scene in the theatre?

2. What action would take place on the stage from the time the scene opens to the time that Lennox says, "May 't please your highness sit"? (Scene 4, line 46)

3. What is Macbeth's reaction to the news he receives from the murderer?

4. From the dialogue, try to visualize the action on stage from the point where Macbeth first sees the ghost of Banquo to the reappearance of the ghost. (lines 57–109) Explain the actions and behavior of Macbeth, Lady Macbeth, and the guests.

5. Try to visualize the stage action that occurs after the ghost reappears (line 109), explaining again the actions and behavior

of Macbeth, Lady Macbeth, and the guests. What is the probable effect of Macbeth's behavior on the assembled guests?

6. Which qualities of Macbeth's character already manifested earlier in the play are revealed again in the banquet scene?

7. What qualities of character does Lady Macbeth evidence in this scene? Comment on the probable inner effects of the role she must play.

8. Macbeth's dialogue with Lady Macbeth when they are alone after the guests have left reveals him further caught up in the nightmare world he has created. In this connection, explain the significance of each of the following passages:

  a. The speech beginning, "It will have blood. . . ." (Scene 4, lines 144—148)

  b. Macbeth's remarks about Macduff. (lines 150—155)

  c. The lines beginning, "I will tomorrow / And betimes I will, to the weird sisters." (lines 155—163)

  d. Macbeth's last words in the scene, beginning "My strange and self-abuse." (lines 165—167)

9. How do you account for the fact that Lady Macbeth seems to have so little to say in the dialogue with Macbeth after the departure of the guests?

10. Does Lennox's first speech in Scene 6 show him to be a supporter of Macbeth, or hostile to him? Support your answer by specific references to the content of the speech.

11. What appears to be the attitude toward Macbeth of the lord with whom Lennox speaks in Scene 6?

12. In general, what do we learn from the dialogue between Lennox and the lord in Scene 6?

SHAKESPEARE'S LANGUAGE AND CRAFT

13. The events of Scene 4 take place at a state banquet, an occasion of brilliantly lit dignity and conviviality. What dramatic effect did Shakespeare achieve by making such a banquet the setting for the events that occur in that scene?

14. Observe the exact sequence of events on the stage in the following instances and show how the use of dramatic irony in each case heightens the tension of the play.

   a. The events that follow Lennox's request that Macbeth take his seat at the table. (Scene 4, lines 46—62)

   b. The events that follow Macbeth's attempt to resume the banquet after the ghost's first exit, beginning with the lines, "I do forget. Do not muse at me. . . ." (lines 99—126)

15. How does the imagery in each of the following passages in Scene 4 serve to vivify or intensify the feelings that are expressed by the speaker? Refer to specific words or lines.

   a. Lady Macbeth's attempt to bring Macbeth out of his state of horror and confusion at the appearance of the ghost. (lines 71—79)

   b. Macbeth's comment on the ghost's appearance which begins, "Blood hath been shed ere now. . . ." (lines 88—96)

   c. Macbeth's cry to the ghost on the latter's second appearance, which begins: "Avaunt! and quit my sight. . . ." (lines 109—112)

16. Compare the opening statement of Macbeth in Scene 4, in which the guests are told how they are to be seated, with the lines Lady Macbeth speaks telling them how they are to depart. (lines 138—140) How does the contrast epitomize and symbolize the kind of world Macbeth has created in his kingdom?

17. Note the two references to the recurring image of blood at the conclusion of Scene 4:

(1)   "It will have blood: they say blood will have blood."

                                                              (line 144)

(2)   ". . . For mine own good
         All causes shall give way: I am in blood
         Stepp'd in so far that, should I wade no more,
         Returning were as tedious as go o'er."

                                                    (lines 158—161)

Explain the significance of the blood references in both passages.

Act IV

THE NIGHTMARE WORLD OF MACBETH

1. The behavior and incantations of the witches in the first part of this act serve as a reminder of the ominous world in which the major action of the play takes place — a world produced by the surrender of Macbeth to his evil impulses. What are some of the details in the behavior and spells of the witches which contribute to this effect?

2. In what ways does Macbeth's speech to the other witches calling on them to respond to his questions show the extent to which he has been driven to monomania (complete obsession with his own evil goals)?

3. Note carefully the first three apparitions which the witches conjure up, and the speeches which these apparitions utter.

    a. What is the exact nature of the apparition in each case?

    b. What statement does each apparition utter?

    c. What is the effect of these statements on Macbeth?

4. As a reader of the play, or as a member of the audience, would you be inclined to share Macbeth's feelings of success on hearing these prophecies, or would you not? Explain why.

5. Describe the fourth apparition that appears to Macbeth. (Note the details as Macbeth describes them in his speech. Scene 1, lines 123–135) What effect does this apparition have? How would you summarize the total effect of the four apparitions?

6. What news does Lennox bring to Macbeth?

7. Note Macbeth's soliloquy on hearing this news. (lines 159–170)

    a. What change from Macbeth's earlier character is indicated in the lines, "The very firstlings of my heart shall be / The firstlings of my hand"?

b. How does the intention he expresses in the next lines about Macduff's family indicate the extent of the change in his character?

8. What impressions of Macduff and of his wife do you get from her dialogue with Ross in Scene 2?

9. What impressions of Scotland under Macbeth's rule do you get from Ross's speech in Scene 2, lines 20—25?

10. In Scene 3, Macduff and Malcolm begin clearly to assume central roles in the play.

a. What is the purpose of Macduff's visit to Malcolm in England?

b. Why does Malcolm hesitate to accept Macduff's offer of assistance?

c. How does Malcolm test Macduff's honesty and integrity?

11. How is Macduff affected by Ross's news about his family? What is revealed of his character?

12. What progress has been made in the campaign to overthrow Macbeth?

13. What is the meaning of Malcolm's statement, "Macbeth / Is ripe for shaking"?

SHAKESPEARE'S LANGUAGE AND CRAFT

14. Visually and audibly, the first scene of Act IV, as rendered on stage, carries a strong dramatic impact.

a. Describe in some detail the scene, the lighting, and the behavior of the witches as you imagine they ought to be presented on stage.

b. The meter in which the witches utter their spells is called trochaic; the beat consists of a series of feet of two syllables, each foot accented on the first syllable ("Thrice the brinded cat hath mew'd"). Comment on the suitability and effect of this rhythmic pattern for the speeches of the witches.

c. How does Shakespeare use various effects of sound in the witches' incantations to heighten his dramatic effect?

15. In Macbeth's speech to the witches, calling on them to tell him his future, how does the imagery he uses intensify the sense of the nightmare world he has made for himself? (Scene 1, lines 51—62)

16. From the very first scene of the play, Shakespeare has artfully introduced a kind of juggling of opposites and contradictions to create a general sense of a world of disorder and confusion. ("When the battle's lost and won". . . "Fair is foul, and foul is fair.")

Careful consideration of the first three apparitions Macbeth sees, together with consideration of the effects their speeches have on him, will reveal to the reader how this sense of confusion is sustained further at this point in the play. What possible contradictions or confusions do you find in the apparitions, their speeches, and their effects on Macbeth?

17. How does the appearance of the fourth apparition further create the effect of a juggling of opposites and contradictions?

18. Scene 2 contains considerable dialogue spoken by Lady Macduff and Macduff's young child, much of which may not be essential to the developing action of the play. What dramatic purpose is served by the inclusion of this dialogue?

19. At the conclusion of Act IV, which of the characters in the play do you think ought to be the one who will finally confront Macbeth and bring him to justice? Think back to earlier scenes in the play and show how Shakespeare, by the end of Act IV, has prepared his audience to single out this character as the one to bring retribution to Macbeth.

Act V, Scenes 1 to 4

THE NIGHTMARE WORLD OF MACBETH

1. In the case of Lady Macbeth's sleepwalking scene, Shakespeare seems to have anticipated, centuries ago, some of the most important psychological findings and insights of our own time, which deal with the symbolic interpretation of dreams and the effects of suppression of deeply buried feelings. Modern psychology holds that mental breakdown is often due to long-suppressed or repressed feelings, and that clues to the causes of such breakdown can be found in dreams. Lady Macbeth's sleepwalking can be viewed as such a dream — a dream in motion, a nightmare being acted out.

a. Consider the following actions of Lady Macbeth in her sleepwalking scene, as described in the words of those who watch her, and explain in terms of modern psychological theory why you think she performs these acts:

(1) "I have seen her rise from her bed . . . take forth paper, fold it, write upon 't, read it, afterwards seal it, and again return to bed." (Scene 1, lines 3—7)

(2) "She has light by her continually; 'tis her command."
(lines 20—21)

(3) "Look, how she rubs her hands." (lines 24—25)

b. Read carefully Lady Macbeth's actual utterances in her sleepwalking scene, beginning with line 32. Note how disjointed and disconnected they seem, as the events in a nightmare are disjointed and unconnected. Some of her statements express symbolically the causes and origins of her present condition. Identify these statements and explain the symbolism.

223

c. Some of Lady Macbeth's utterances appear to be repetitions of words she actually must have spoken. Identify these utterances and indicate when she probably spoke these words in the past.

d. In the light of her behavior and utterances in the sleepwalking scene, how would you finally explain the causes of her breakdown? Explain also why you think she, rather than Macbeth himself, broke down in this fashion.

2. What do we learn in Scene 2 of Act V about the military situation in the war to unseat Macbeth?

3. What conclusions about Macbeth's state of mind can you draw from his speeches and behavior in Scene 3? Does he seem to feel secure or insecure as the opposing armies approach? Consider the significance of each of the following passages in your response.

a. The passage beginning, "Bring me no more reports. . . ." (lines 1–10)

b. His words and behavior toward the servant who brings news about the approach of the English. (lines 11–21)

c. His soliloquy beginning, "I am sick at heart. . . ." (lines 22–31)

d. His statement, "I'll fight, till from my bones my flesh be hack'd." (line 37)

e. His order to Seyton, "Hang those who talk of fear." (line 41)

f. His conversation with the doctor about medicine and disease.

g. His final statement:

> "I will not be afraid of death and bane
> Till Birnam forest come to Dunsinane."

(lines 68–69)

4. What plan of battle does Malcolm announce in Scene 4? What appears to be the best strategy for Macbeth, as Malcolm himself states it?

SHAKESPEARE'S LANGUAGE AND CRAFT

5. With rare exceptions, the entire play has been composed in verse, the poetry serving to heighten and intensify the feelings expressed and the effect of the events unfolded. The entire sleepwalking scene (Scene 1), however, with the exception of the doctor's last remarks, is composed in prose. In the light of the situation itself and Shakespeare's purpose, why do you suppose he chose to use prose?

6. There is a subtle and deeply touching dramatic irony in the content of many of the utterances of Lady Macbeth which allude to actual statements she must have made earlier to her husband.

    a. Keeping in mind her original intention, explain the ultimate irony in her repeating the following statements in her sleepwalking scene:

    (1) "Fie, my lord, fie! a soldier and afeard? What need we fear who knows it, when none can call our power to account?"

                               (lines 33—35)

    (2) "No more o' that, my lord, no more o' that: you mar all with this starting." (lines 40—42)

    (3) "Wash your hands; put on your nightgown; look not so pale." (lines 56—57)

    b. Find two other, similar utterances of Lady Macbeth and explain the pathetic irony in each case.

7. In the following instances in Act V, Scenes 2 and 4, there is a sequence of references to Birnam and Dunsinane. How does this sequence show Shakespeare's skill in plot construction? Consider the reactions of the audience and reader as the references appear in sequence.

    (1)   "Near Birnam wood
         Shall we meet them. . . ." (lines 6—7)

    (2)   "Great Dunsinane he strongly fortifies." (line 4)

(3) "Make we our march towards Birnam." (line 37)

(4) "What wood is this before us?"

"Let every soldier hew him down a bough,
And bear 't before him. . . ."   (lines 4, 6—7)

8. Earlier in the play we noted the symbolic importance of Shakespeare's recurrent use of blood imagery. How is this symbolic significance further sustained in the following parts of Lady Macbeth's sleepwalking scene?

a. "Yet here's a spot. . . . Out, damned spot! out, I say!" (Scene 1, lines 29, 32)

b. "Yet who would have thought the old man to have had so much blood in him?" (lines 35—37)

c. "Here's the smell of the blood still: all the perfumes of Arabia will not sweeten this little hand."   (lines 46—47)

9. Comment on the image in the following statement of Angus about Macbeth. Relate it to other significant imagery in the play.

"Now does he feel
His secret murders sticking on his hands."

(Scene 2, lines 19—20)

10. Earlier in the play, attention was called to the recurrent use of clothing imagery in connection with Macbeth. Note Angus's statement in Scene 2 and comment on its significance:·

". . . now does he feel his title
Hang loose about him, like a giant's robe
Upon a dwarfish thief."   (lines 23—25)

11. Macbeth's soliloquy beginning "I am sick at heart. . ." (Act V, Scene 3, lines 22—31) is one of the most moving in the play.

a. Explain the significance of the key metaphor, "my way of life / Is fallen into the sear [dry], the yellow leaf," as it applies to Macbeth at this point in the play. What does it reveal about him?

b. In speaking of the disenchanting reality of his life as king Macbeth says he receives "mouth-honor" and "breath." Explain the meaning of this figurative language

12. A new set of recurrent images is appropriately introduced in the last act; these are images of disease, medicine, and health. Identify such imagery in each of the following passages and explain its appropriateness and significance at this stage in the play:

a. The remarks of Caithness announcing the movement of the rebel army toward Birnam. (Scene 2, lines 32—34) The image is in these lines:

> "Meet we the medicine of the sickly weal,
> And with him pour we, in our country's purge,
> Each drop of us."

b. The remarks of Macbeth to the doctor concerning relief for Lady Macbeth's condition. (Scene 3, lines 46—52)

c. Macbeth's further remarks on disease and medicine beginning, "If thou couldst, doctor, cast / The water of my land. . . ." (Scene 3, lines 58—64)

13. Growth in nature — the appearance of trees and greenery — has always served in myth and literature as a symbol of renewed life and vitality, an allusion to the spring season in the cycle of nature. In the light of this fact, what possible new significance do you see in the third apparition that appeared to Macbeth in Act IV — "a Child crowned, with a tree in his hand"? What extension of this symbolism may there be in Malcolm's plan to have his army approach Dunsinane carrying the boughs of trees?

Act V, Scenes 5 to 8

THE NIGHTMARE WORLD OF MACBETH

1. The first scenes of the last act have indicated that the nightmare world created by Macbeth's first evil act is drawing to a close. The striking shifts of mood in Macbeth's speeches are prompted by the rapid succession of events in the last scenes.

Note the alternations of mood as they appear in the following speeches of Macbeth, and explain these shifts in the light of the events as they occur.

a. The speech beginning, "Hang out our banners on the outward walls. . . ." (Scene 5, lines 1—7)

b. The speech beginning, "I have almost forgot the taste of fears. . . ." (lines 10—16) Compare these remarks with his earlier soliloquy in Act I (Scene 3, lines 138—150) in which he describes how he reacts to the contemplation of the possible murder of Duncan.

c. The speech beginning, "She should have died hereafter. . . ." (Scene 5, lines 19—30)

d. The speech beginning, "If thou speak'st false. . . ." (Scene 5, lines 43—57)

e. Macbeth's successive speeches before and during his encounter with Young Siward. (Scene 7)

f. Macbeth's successive remarks to Macduff when they finally encounter one another. (Scene 8)

2. In what way does the conclusion of the play serve to dissipate the sense of nightmare that has prevailed? Note, in this connection, Malcolm's last speech. (Scene 8, lines 71—86)

3. Malcolm calls Macbeth "this dead butcher," and most readers will agree that Macbeth's fate has been deserved. Did Shakespeare want us to view Macbeth exactly as Malcolm views him, or did he want us to have a different feeling about him? In your response, refer to the character and behavior of Macbeth as you have known him throughout the play.

4. a. What explanation does Malcolm offer for the death of Lady Macbeth?

b. Malcolm characterizes Lady Macbeth as a "fiend-like queen." Do you accept this characterization? Explain your answer.

5. Where do you think Shakespeare wanted us to lay the primary responsibility for Macbeth's course of evil — on the witches? on Lady Macbeth? on himself? Review the events of the play in considering your answer.

SHAKESPEARE'S LANGUAGE AND CRAFT

6. Despite Macbeth's manifest villainy, many readers at the close of the play retain some measure of sympathy and respect for him. How does Shakespeare's presentation of his thoughts and actions in the last scenes serve to make the reader retain such a measure of sympathy and respect? Refer specifically to the lines that have this effect.

7. Throughout the play we have observed how Shakespeare's repeated use of antithesis and paradox has been a factor in sustaining the sense of a nightmare world in which opposites and contradictions prevail over order and regularity. In each of these speeches of Macbeth, identify the antithesis or paradox and explain its significance:

a. The speech in which Macbeth responds to the announcement that Birnam wood seems to be moving to Dunsinane. (Scene 5, lines 43–57)

b. The speech in which Macbeth responds to Macduff's announcement that he was "from his mother's womb untimely ripp'd." (Scene 8, lines 21–26)

8. The soliloquy beginning, "I have almost forgot the taste of fears" (Scene 5, lines 10–16), reveals an important change in Macbeth's character which is expressed through a series of striking metaphors. Trace these metaphors, and show how they build up to express the change Macbeth is describing.

9. The most memorable soliloquy in the play is that which begins "Tomorrow, and tomorrow, and tomorrow." (Scene 5, lines 21–30)

a. What general feeling about life is expressed in this soliloquy?

b. The philosophy of life in this soliloquy is expressed in a series of four central metaphors.

(1) The first metaphor (lines 21–23) comments on the nature of time and history as Macbeth perceives it. What are the key words in this metaphor and how do they work to express the meaning? How does the movement or rhythm of the lines also help to convey the meaning?

(2) The second metaphor (lines 24–25) introduces a new image and a new comment derived from the first. What is life compared to in these lines? What comment about its character is made?

(3) The third and fourth metaphors serve to elaborate why Macbeth feels that life ought to be extinguished. Identify the metaphors that conclude the soliloquy and explain their significance.

c. The thoughts expressed in this soliloquy have aroused considerable comment and controversy. Do they represent Shakespeare's own feelings about life and its meaning? Are they only the thoughts a man who has lived through the experiences of Macbeth would have, unique to him and the circumstances of his life? Or is there a universal quality in these thoughts, a significance and relevance that go beyond Macbeth's situation and touch all of us? Discuss the content of this soliloquy from the point of view of these questions.

10. Comment on the manner in which Shakespeare constructed the conclusion of the play. Why do you think the ending was either suitable or unsatisfactory?